OPEN TO
QUESTION

Walter L. Bateman

OPEN TO
QUESTION

The Art of Teaching
and Learning by Inquiry

Foreword by William G. Perry, Jr.

 Jossey-Bass Publishers

San Francisco   •   Oxford   •   1990

OPEN TO QUESTION
The Art of Teaching and Learning by Inquiry
by Walter L. Bateman

Copyright © 1990 by: Jossey-Bass Inc., Publishers
350 Sansome Street
San Francisco, California 94104
&
Jossey-Bass Limited
Headington Hill Hall
Oxford OX3 0BW

Library of Congress Cataloging-in-Publication Data

Bateman, Walter L.
    Open to question : the art of teaching and learning by inquiry /
Walter L. Bateman.
        p.   cm.—(The Jossey-Bass higher education series) (The
Jossey-Bass education series)
    Includes bibliographical references and index.
    ISBN 1-55542-268-3
    1. College teaching.   2. Teaching.   3. Inquiry (Theory of
knowledge)   I. Title.   II. Series.   III. Series: The Jossey-Bass
education series.
LB2331.B377   1990
378.1′25—dc20
                                                90-53089
                                                    CIP

Manufactured in the United States of America

The paper in this book meets the guidelines for
permanence and durability of the Committee on
Production Guidelines for Book Longevity of the
Council on Library Resources.

JACKET DESIGN BY CHARLOTTE KAY
JACKET ILLUSTRATION BY JOHN HERSEY

FIRST EDITION

Code 9086

A joint publication in

The Jossey-Bass
Higher Education Series

and

The Jossey-Bass Education Series

Consulting Editor
Adult and Continuing Education

ALAN B. KNOX
University of Wisconsin, Madison

CONTENTS

FOREWORD

This is a delightful book, and important. Learning through inquiry has been described before, but never so vividly. *Open to Question* is addressed to teachers, of course; but if formal teaching has not been part of your fate, you will be delighted and informed.

Walter Bateman writes to be read with ease. His humor and invention carry the weight of his message lightly. He finds ways to let you enter into the very sense of discovery that his students experience. You may find yourself pausing to ponder a fresh vision of your own ways of learning important things, not only as a student or a teacher but as a citizen of the world. In Chapter Thirteen, Bateman shares such a learning of his own.

One might suppose that a description of discovery and learning so vivid and recognizable would need no theoretical justification. Bateman, however, does refer to the research of Piaget on students' thinking and pays me the honor of citing some of my own. I return the favor here by citing a particular example that supports Bateman's bold understanding of the hierarchy in students' motivations. This confirmation comes in the form of an anecdote told me by the great Canadian psychologist Donald Hebb. Hebb was fond of saying that a certain encounter with a student early in his teaching had determined the direction of all his research and building of theories, especially of his theory of pleasure. The student's name was Mona, and she was a chimpanzee.

At the time of the event, Hebb was part of a team at the Yerkes Laboratory in Florida studying complex learning in primates. The team had designed steplike series of increasingly complicated puzzles ingeniously built into latches. The latches opened see-through grille doors that could be mounted on a box containing food. It was now the turn of Mona, known in similar experiments for her dependable scholastic aptitude.

Hebb paused here in his account to recall that in those days the "subject" in any psychological experiment in learning was required to be "motivated." There were three scientifically respectable motives: hunger, sex, and fear. Now, too much use of fear had troubling by-products, and sex was notoriously unstable, but an animal could easily be motivated by hunger. Mona had accordingly been put on a reduced diet until she became irritable and demanding and had lost a bit of weight; she was then declared scientifically motivated. She was placed on a stool facing the box. The box was closed by the first door with its puzzle-latch. In plain sight within the box lay a banana. The experimenters readied their stopwatches and tally sheets.

Mona was quick to discover the secret of this first latch. She opened the door, reached for the banana, peeled it, and suddenly paused. A flaw had appeared in the experimental procedure. The experimenters had been careful to keep the rest of the bananas out of Mona's sight; it had not occurred to them to sequester the rest of the doors. These doors, with their intriguing latches, lay on the floor and caught Mona's eye. She broke a small piece off the top of her banana, placed it on top of the box, put the rest of the banana back in the box, and signaled for the next door. She went through the whole series of doors, intent and skillful, each time placing another piece of the banana on top of the box in a geometrical pattern—her tally sheet.

After Mona dispatched the last door, the team congratulated her, gave her the other bananas, and collected their gear to depart. It was then that Mona underlined the lesson of the day. She jumped screaming onto Hebb's shoulder, pulled his hair, and demanded that the team return and start over while she unlocked each of those puzzles once again, putting the pieces of the banana one by one back into the box.

To translate this event into the classrooms that Bateman is describing, for "bananas" read "grades." In keeping with Mona's priorities, Bateman hardly mentions grades.

He does, apparently, give "spot quizzes" and provide other such conventional structures as students need in order to know where they stand. His students are in special need of such assurances, for Bateman intrigues them with puzzle-latches on doors. The students may start out looking for grades, but when they open the door they find wonder. Wonder and more latches.

Such wonder can be great fun and very frightening. Passionate inquiry can lead to terror. Does every answer lead to another question? Are there no answers to memorize that are *surely* right? Has life's picture no frame? Bateman is aware that for some even the more conventional rituals are not enough. To the few who retreat in anger he accords respect. To those who falter in confusion he offers imaginative and compassionate support. His account of such a moment is touching.

For the majority, Bateman's invitation to inquire offers an opportunity for metamorphosis. Intrigued by their discoveries, they abandon the chrysalis of pupilhood to exercise their powers as students.

If you teach, you may wonder as you read, "Yes, but how can I find the time to prepare all the materials? I'm really tired covering the entire syllabus, as it is!" But you already know the feeling when a class takes hold; it carries you with it. When pupils are passive, they drain you; when students are involved, they give back your energies with joy—Bateman's word.

Watertown, Massachusetts   William G. Perry, Jr.
August 1990

PREFACE

Is this book valuable enough to justify chopping down a tree? Are the ideas new?

They are valuable but not new. Teaching by inquiry is very ancient. From John Dewey back to Socrates, many have urged this kind of teaching; thousands of good teachers already use the inductive approach. No, I present nothing original, but the approach is very valuable.

My first justification for chopping down that tree is that this book differs from most of its predecessors: It is readable. It is utterly free of jargon. Well, almost utterly. You should find it fun to read, even exciting, if you can believe that about any book on teaching.

The problem with the method of inquiry is that not enough teachers use it, not enough understand the power inherent in provocative inquiry, not enough see their job as other than transmitting knowledge. They have knowledge; students get it. Teachers know; students learn. Teachers talk; students listen and once in a while even take notes.

The approach of inquiry shifts the emphasis to a far more active role for the student than just that of a passive soaker-up of information, soaker-up of new vocabulary, soaker-up of correct interpretations, soaker-up of the Truth. Here the student becomes the groper, the one who tests her guesses, the one who asks questions pertinent to his needs and then searches for answers, learning lots of intellectual skills along the route. The route is one of maturation and the discarding of old mental patterns to replace them with newer and more functional patterns.

My second justification for the chopping down of a beautiful green tree is that this book uses the method that it describes. Each chapter not only includes the conversations of learners groping for meaning but loops the reader into that same search. Almost every chapter begins with the data needed to solve a problem, the clues needed to work out the puzzle. You, too, can have the fun of thinking.

Children love to ask riddles. But you disappoint them when you respond with the answer. For the young child, telling you the answer is half the fun. For the older child, thinking out the answer is all the fun. Many of our teachers deprive their students of the fun of thinking out the answer. They want the fun of telling the answer themselves, the fun of delivering the lecture, the fun of talking and talking and talking.

When Lech Walesa, onetime shipyard electrician, spoke to the U.S. Congress in 1989, he asked directly for help for Poland. "I must tell you that the supply of words on the world market is plentiful, but the demand is falling. Let deeds follow words now."

This book is aimed at teachers in college and in high school and in junior high and possibly in elementary school, but elementary teaching is too important for a novice like me to mess around with. I have used these methods in junior high, in senior high, in college, and in adult seminars. I know they work. As a volunteer teacher of archaeology to one group of sixth-grade students, I can vouch for methods of inquiry's working there, too.

Open to Question is also aimed at parents. If this type of teaching is what you want for your children, tell the teacher. Give her the book. It may well be the highest praise you can offer a competent teacher. Talk to the school board about this type of teaching and how it will help students to mature and to think critically. Our country desperately needs mature citizens who can think critically. Democracy is the form of government that requires criticism and debate among its citizens.

The book is also aimed at the growing group of teachers and

administrators who mentor that growing group of adults returning to college, many of them A.C. or A.D.—after children or after divorce.

I seek new converts; I try to inflame tired passions. Teachers using inquiry may find nourishment for renewal here, encouragement to teach even better.

First, my message is clear and readable; second, the inductive method advocated is used on the reader so that you share the fun of thinking much as a student would. Those two reasons form my *apologia pro libro meo* to justify putting the ax to that tree.

What Is Covered?

The three chapters forming the first part (Question One) illustrate the change in students when inquiry/inductive methods are used; they show how conflict over ideas can stimulate learning and growth. And they reveal the excitement and the pain that a student undergoes in dropping an old idea, in shedding an old skin.

The bulk of the chapters fall in the second part (Question Two). The examples offered illustrate classroom conversations about students groping to unravel a mystery, to solve a problem. These ten chapters range over several disciplines. Most of them reflect my personal experience in teaching history, sociology, and anthropology; a few are taken from other teachers and other disciplines.

The third part (Question Three) recapitulates how you as the teacher must reshape your own role and how you can organize lessons of inquiry. Finally, I warn that some people do not want students to think or teachers to challenge. I close with the delights of dealing with students who grow and learn and manage to think freely.

Omission: My text may give the impression that I began with sound educational theory and worked out my method from that. Nonsense. Every winter, I had two or three flu infections that left me with laryngitis. Frustrated by my feeble croaking, I wrote general questions on the board and led discussions by pointing with a ruler and writing more questions. Bringing in contradictory texts provided for a genuine struggle over ideas. The system evolved and was rationalized later.

The unspeakable teacher was forced to create a different system. I reinvented an old method. It worked to push my students to play an active role in their own learning.

Obligations and Thanks

Thanks to my best teachers; out of many, a special few: Mira Southworth, David Lynch, Walter S. Campbell.

Many thanks to those friends who have criticized various chapters: Janeth Mathison, Mary Elizabeth Olsen, Cecelia Gulson, and Patricia Calvert; Mary Goette criticized every chapter. And many thanks to those friendly librarians who helped so patiently.

Thanks also to Daniel Kelly, former editor of *Minnesota Monthly,* where Chapter Five appeared in November 1988 as a Tamarack Award–winning essay. Dan taught me once again how cutting improves writing. And dozens of readers of *Minnesota Monthly* encouraged me with their responses, especially Larry Copes of Augsburg College.

Thanks to the editorial criticism and commentary and cheering on of Laurent Parks Daloz and William Perry and Alan Knox and the staff at Jossey-Bass.

Most thanks to Sue, friendly critic, dogged proofreader, mother of our children, USO director, parasailor, investor, wine bottle washer, volunteer, humorist, bridge player, YWCA executive, river rafter, composer of doggerel, climber to high places, companion and confidante and wife, who has wrenched precious time from her graduate studies to egg me on and who has let me use our Apple IIc as long as it did not interfere with her dedicated scramble to finish her master's degree before we turn seventy-six.

Plenty of folks gave me suggestions, advice, and criticism. Since I adopted only what I understood, any errors remaining must be doubly mine.

Thanks to about twelve thousand students who struggled through my classes while I was learning to teach. Some of you discovered what I was trying to do; now I shall confess to the rest. Your responses helped me to learn, as you will now discover. Let me remind you that I never gave one of you a grade; you earned it.

I remember with pleasure your curiosity and grit as I dedicate this book to all my students.

Rochester, Minnesota   Walter L. Bateman
August 1990

THE AUTHOR

Walter L. Bateman, who was born in Duluth, Minnesota, in 1916, earned his B.A. in sociology from the University of Chicago in 1937 and his M.A. in history from the University of Minnesota in 1942. Since then he has studied anthropology and other perspectives on human behavior at various universities: Mexico, Paris, Denver, Oklahoma, Oregon, Hamline, Minnesota, Wisconsin, and Indiana.

From 1942 to 1946 his education was enriched in the infantry, specifically in a heavy-weapons company, with exciting field trips to France and Germany. In 1947 he took a post at what is now Rochester Community College in Rochester, Minnesota, teaching anthropology, sociology, and history, later adding human sexuality and aging to broaden his qualifications as a "generalist."

After serving as chair of the Division of Social Sciences for several years, he stepped down to enhance his own satisfaction and that of others, thus doubly validating the Peter Principle. Although this role model failed to secure emulation, one latent function was more time for writing.

He has written several books: in 1965, *How Our Government Began* (with Fred King) and, in 1966, *How Man Began*. Both were supplementary readers for junior high schools. In 1970, for the Unitarian Universalist Association, he designed and wrote a multimedia curriculum, *Man the Culture Builder*, including two books— *The Navajo of the Painted Desert* and *The Kung of the Kalahari*—

as well as two guides for teaching by inquiry. He has also written about 144 articles of a popular nature on such topics as city planning, police training, archaeology, and Minnesota history.

In 1943 he married the woman described too briefly in the preface. They have three children, now grown. Since retiring in 1981, he has devoted his time to chess, photography, writing, growing roses, making wine, reading all of Shakespeare and a bunch of detective novels, serving as guardian ad litem or courtroom advocate for abused and neglected children and, recently, as a peer counselor in Elder Network. He and his wife travel when they can, with recent sightings reported in Armenia, Avignon, the Azores, Beijing, Belém, Cairo, Canterbury, Chinandega, Dunhuang, and Duluth. His written plans on file for his memorial service detail explicitly the speakers, the musicians, the exhibits, and the quality of refreshment.

OPEN TO QUESTION

WHY TEACH BY INQUIRY?

Chapters One and Two illustrate the excitement that can develop in a classroom when inductive or inquiry measures permit the students to puzzle over problems, to elicit rules, or to evaluate choices.

Chapter Three shows the value in helping students reconstruct their naive mental patterns toward more mature patterns via the theories of Jean Piaget and William Perry, Jr. The method is disequilibrium; the cost comes in discomfort; the reward is maturation and growth in critical abilities plus a wonderful eagerness to learn more. A license to think becomes a permit to grow.

1

Why Don't They Take Notes?

3 Oct 88

Dear Jack,

Your history class was a delight. You lectured and handled questions superbly, far better than I recall doing it when I first taught in college after the war.

Your students certainly respect you. And you respect yourself for being well prepared, and that confidence sure does shine through. However, I'll just bet that the first time you were as clammy-fingered as I was when I began teaching in a college jammed with veterans on the GI Bill. Four years in the infantry left me feeling that I had forgotten all the books. Every night I boned up.

Boning up. I must have taken full notes on at least two books every week for that first year.

I kept a journal trying to learn how to teach. Finally, I came up with four qualities of a good teacher. Confidence was first. If I did not know something, I found out. But en route, I discovered that when someone threw me a difficult question, it was no sin to admit that I didn't know. The sin came in the next class when I still didn't know. After I had researched some ques-

3

tion, I always answered that student in the next class and practically made him take notes on my answer and my source.

Slowly I learned a better way.

Student asks question. Teacher grins. "I'm not sure, but I'll tell you on Friday. I'll give you a nickel if you find out before I do."

The very first time I tried that, the student accepted my challenge. She came back to class and read off her notes. Then I read off mine. Our different sources largely agreed. I searched for a nickel, marched back to her desk, and presented it with a grand flourish. The class applauded. She got red, happy red.

From then on, it was much easier for me to admit ignorance. Whenever a student failed to search, everyone groaned.

Now my roundabout reason for recalling this story is that you fielded three questions and you answered two of them very directly. The third was "Why does our history text say that General Potemkin was only a mediocre general?"

I noticed that you hesitated and then launched into slightly bawdy stories of Potemkin as lover of Catherine the Great, and then told a humorous yarn about Potemkin villages, and by then the period was up. Exit laughing.

May I recommend the nickel technique? Even when you do know the answer, it won't hurt once in a while to say that you're not sure. The kids will love you.

In addition to confidence, you also have another key ingredient. You have enthusiasm. You love what you teach. It is a delight to listen to you, because what shines through is that you really want us to know as much history as you do.

Wonderful. A teacher should feel that his subject is the most important and exciting field of knowledge in the world.

A bored and listless teacher does unbelievable damage to students. Better to quit. You teach your attitude.

In your office, I noticed many books other than free textbooks. You buy books, and that too is a measure of enthusiasm: the amount of your own money you spend on your books and your journals.

Confidence and enthusiasm are essential.

That was great to see you in action. Thanks once more. I hope to visit again in about four weeks.

Your admiring uncle,

Walter

*   *   *

October 17, 1988

Dear Walter,

Thanks for that long and fascinating letter; I'm glad that you enjoyed my class.

But with your assumptions regarding my memory of General Potemkin's military accomplishments and the reason for the somewhat slighting reference to him in the text I really must disagree. That he had bungled badly in one particular military operation of 1787 against the Turks, failing to reinforce his troops and failing to provide sufficient supplies, I knew very well. Had he not been a favorite of the empress or had there been more adequate officers available, either one of these should have been sufficient cause to replace him. This lack marked the czarist army of the period in many ways, making it comparable to later Russian armies, most of which have been poorly led and miserably equipped, with the untrained peasants bearing the brunt of dying of their untreated wounds while their high officers lived regally like Sultans.

No, the real reason was that the clock showed three minutes left; my material on the military campaign fitted far better in the subsequent lecture, when I gave General Potemkin the treatment he deserved.

However, your suggestion of my pretending ignorance in order to persuade some totally untrained novice to delve into books that she could barely read and could scarcely comprehend smacks of a dereliction of the duties of a teacher. All things in good time; one must learn to walk before one learns to run. More than that, to pretend ignorance in order to lure a student to visit the library I find personally distasteful. What are they doing in college? Why are their parents paying these enormous amounts of money? My mission is to teach history, not to coddle. The library stands open, waiting, filled with marvels; failing to use it becomes their dereliction.

Your letter promised to elucidate four major characteristics of the competent teacher; you delivered on only a moiety of the promise; I trust that you will not fail to clarify the remaining two.

Your presence was welcome; your next visit is awaited; perhaps I could lure you into giving a lecture on a topic germane to the period we are studying. Should this appeal to you, you might schedule your visit to coincide with one of your favorite topics listed in my class schedule of lectures, which I am enclosing.

Historically,

Jack

*   *   *

30 Oct 88

Dear Jack,

Back home safely, but my knees still feel squeezed from those tight rows on the plane.

That second visit was as entertaining as the first. I envy you. You organize a magnificent lecture, complete with humor that is appropriate and advances your argument, not the silly joke telling with which some people fill up time. I'm sorry we could not talk long afterward, but plane schedules are demanding, and you had that next class.

However and but. Since I seem to be playing the role of critic, I might as well tell you what your visiting spy saw from the back row where I perched myself.

Here's my tally of those that I could see who had also chosen seats way back.

Studying French: 3 women
Writing letters: 2 women, 1 man
Studying other textbooks: 6 men, 1 woman
Writing a list (groceries?):   1 woman

Of the 15 others I could see, all listened, but only 3 took notes. And you probably have as high a percentage as anyone. Those who sit up front are the eager ones, and they take notes, sometimes even good notes.

I wrestled with note-taking forty years ago. I tried threats. I tried checking their notes. Finally I asked them directly. My students told me that there was no point to taking notes because my tests covered the textbook only, never the lectures.

So I widened my tests to include the lectures. That helped a little. Then I changed my lectures.

Instead of supplementing the text, I argued with it. A textbook writer has to choose which interpretation he is going to use and often picks the bland one. Bland poses least risk of upsetting some parent. I remember that we were in a class on U.S. history just after the Revolution, getting into the Constitution.

For years my students had read patriotic puffery about the brilliance of the founding fathers. True, they were brilliant and farsighted. But when you read their biographies, you notice that they were also men with feelings of greed and lust and pride. They each wanted to defend their own turf; nobody wanted to give power to the other guy. The true brilliance came in the compromises they worked out; what we call democracy rose partially from the compromises.

I lectured from Charles Beard. I gave them an idea of who those guys were in terms of land holdings and wealth and slaves. I gave them a picture of bright men arguing for their own welfare, compromising a bit, and thus developing a system with checks and balances wherein the other men from other states could not readily gang up on them. But they all agreed to keep the power to themselves; the working class and all the women were cut out of the power system almost as much as the slaves.

Suddenly my class was arguing with me. It unsettled them to think of great men as being like other men. It unsettled them to think that persuasions of power and greed such as we have today would have operated back in that paradise of 1787. The argument stirred the class. They paid attention. They took notes. They were disturbed. Even the back row came alive, partly.

To get them to review for the exam, I used to give ten essay questions in advance, then pick out three of them on exam day. One was to compare that lecture with the text and then to justify a conclusion. They wanted to talk about that question. We had a magnificent discussion, with students on both sides. Even the back row began copying notes from the front row.

I had learned one big lesson. If you give students conflicting interpretations, they get to use their big, bright brains. They are smarter than we think. But we seldom encourage them to do anything but memorize.

Then I had to learn another lesson even harder. But enough for now, I'll explain it later.

Sorry I misjudged your total recall on Potemkin. But the nickel idea is still a good one.

With nostalgia,

Walter

*   *   *

Armistice Day 88

Dear Walter,

Thank you for the report on those who pay attention in class and those who are serious enough to take notes. Of course, I can't see what they are doing; but the response to a bit of humor is either absent from the back benches or seems forced and late. We are all aware that many students bring their bodies into class, but not always their minds; all sorts of pressures occupy them, from sports to money problems to love affairs to sick children. Our faculty's usual response is that students pay the tuition and they can choose to leave the product behind after they have paid; a free country permits choices in many areas, even self-damaging choices.

Your proposal of presenting a conflicting point of view interests me; in any period of history, a varying inter-

pretation would be easy to find. Ever since receiving your letter, I've been thinking up ways to challenge the class; however, one insurmountable problem prevents me: Most of them do not read assignments regularly. They postpone study and then cram for a test; consequently, should I subtly contradict a chapter that most of them have not yet read, my effort would fail. Only a few would perceive what had happened. Of those, most would hesitate to raise the issue; instead, they would passively take notes.

Well, sir, you did deliver on your third point: the use of conflict to stimulate interest. However, I still await the fourth quality of a good teacher as you saw it.

Yours,

Jack

          *   *   *   *

27 November 88

Dear Jack,

Did I really write that I had four qualities of a good teacher? Some years there were six or sixteen. But I kept combining until the number was smaller.

My point number three was not clearly stated. What I should have written was to have faith in the student's ability to think. When we teachers met over coffee, we would often trade yarns about stupid remarks and stupid papers and preen ourselves because we knew more than freshmen. So let me state it clearly. The teacher must have confidence and enthusiasm and faith in students' brains. Whether you use conflict or challenge or puzzles or problems is a matter of technique.

The fourth point was that lesson I learned when I did manage to get students arguing and discussing. I had to learn to slow down the lecturing and to play a different role. I had to develop new skills of encouraging opinions, and encouraging the testing of ideas against documents, and encouraging the shy ones to speak up, of countering the loudmouths with the factual opinion of another student.

After years of practice in delivering some pretty slick lectures, I had to learn to shut up, to encourage alternate opinions, to get them to decide which answer better fit the facts, to keep them on track but not to tell them which I thought had the better answer.

Darned few of them had ever had the opportunity before. School was the place where you went to hear the truth. And when I slowly and grudgingly realized that they would learn better if I stepped back, they blossomed.

Well, some did. They had much to learn as well. They had to learn to discuss and to propose an answer that might seem silly and to make a judgment about another student's answer. Their world of school slowly turned upside down. Instead of being given a lot of Truth to memorize, they were faced with choices and decisions and defensive arguments. Maybe the old world of school had been upside down and we were turning it the right way up.

I like to think that. The learning came not just in memorizing facts, but in mastering the skills of thinking as well as critical attitudes. Such skills would last them a lot longer. My fourth quality for the good teacher was to learn the skills needed to get students to think critically.

The teacher should stay out of the discussion. Stand back. Shut up on the lecture. Encourage students to speak. Be a cheerleader, not a judge. And that lesson was much harder for me to learn, because it went against the grain of all my practice; for years I had studied and organized clever and brilliant lectures, and now much of my class time was being "wasted" on student talk, with often endless arguments over the same point by stubborn adherents.

Someplace in there I caught on that "wasting time" was the error in my thinking. The students were spending time in a training ground by handling evidence and handling logic and handling persuasion and thus learning how history gets written. No waste there. By giving them a choice of interpretation, I was learning to do inductive teaching, or teaching by inquiry.

And another thing happened. Of course, developing wholly new lectures takes time, so obviously I still used mostly old ones that were pretty good. But once those kids had tasted blood, they liked the taste. My next lecture was bland stuff, nothing exciting. They didn't believe it. They argued with it. Two of them went to the library and found cases to question my stand. They had become the challengers.

Never did I dare tell them that my lecture was intended to be the Truth and not to be challenged.

Well, Jack, I finally delivered on the four points and may have irritated you in the delivery. Please test these out and argue with me just as I urged my students to argue.

Inquiringly,

Walter

P.S. You got me started. I'm actually trying to write down some of the teaching techniques that worked. I shall send some along, and you can have fun tearing them apart. And if they make sense, maybe I can publish something on the method called discovery teaching or inductive teaching or teaching by inquiry.

*　　　　*　　　　*

December 15, 1988

Dear Walter,

Thank you for that long letter, which puts to shame this brief reply; but everything comes in a rush this week just before Christmas. Much as I enjoy your stories, I feel that different techniques of teaching work for different teachers. You surely have tried many.

Why call it inductive teaching, when Sherlock Holmes used deductive logic with such great effect? What is the difference, and why should one be preferred? Never have I heard of lectures as deductive teaching.

Writing down your experiences is a superb idea, and should you really want a friendly critic who is not afraid to criticize or disagree, please send me some chapters. I promise to criticize tactfully and cheerfully.

Hastily and Merry Christmas,

Jack

*　　　　*　　　　*

Happy New Year
4 Jan 89

Dear Jack,

I'm having a ball in looking through old notebooks and old textbooks and trying to organize. Just a couple of hasty answers.
Inductive means you start with data and draw a

generalization that explains and gives meaning to your data.

Deductive means that you take that generalization and apply it to new stuff.

Sherlock once studied dozens of kinds of tobacco ash and drew some generalizations: inductive thinking. But when he was on a case and found some ash, he applied his general rules to the specific case: deductive thinking. He used both types; inductive must come first.

What you do when you lecture is better called exposition.

To get my students to study each day instead of cramming, I used to give short pop quizzes, usually objective and corrected immediately in class. If I had time, I gave them a brief essay. The unannounced quiz definitely keeps students studying each day; that way, you can plan your lecture to conflict with the text knowing that most of them will come prepared. And that way you can get them thinking, using those big brains.

I hope to send a few chapters soon. I'm having fun. Carry on.

Walter

2

Telling or Showing?

The students read the description carefully.

"The skeleton of an adult male *Homo sapiens* was lying on the right side, curled up, knees to chest. The bones and the surrounding soil were stained reddish with ochre, powdered iron ore. Near the head were two stone knives, one stone spearhead, and the hindquarter bones of a reindeer, scratched as if from the stone knife. The date was approximately 15,000 years before the present. The bones were quite similar to those of a modern human being. The dig was in the floor of a cave."

The teacher waited. The class hesitated briefly before launching into speculations. Then they came, often disagreeing with each other.

"They buried their dead."

"That means that they believed in an afterlife."

"Some sort of heaven or nice place."

"They thought the dead would need weapons and tools."

"Makes it sound like a Happy Hunting Ground."

"At least they thought the weapons would be useful."

"Why were the bones colored red?"

"Were the reindeer bones red also?"

"Those reindeer bones could have been left as food."

Teacher: "Whoa, down a bit. Let's take items one at a time. What do you make of the knives and spear?"

"Maybe they thought of some sort of Happy Hunting Ground where they would be needed in an afterlife."

"That sounds good to me."

"Well, perhaps, but maybe this guy got killed while hunting and nobody wanted his weapons because they might bring bad luck. Didn't we read about some tribe that were miserably poor because every time someone died, they destroyed all his possessions and burned his house?"

"Yeah, we called that a dysfunctional norm. I remember that, because ever since I've been collecting dysfunctional norms. I love that phrase."

"If the reindeer bone was meant for food, then that would support the afterlife notion."

"Maybe that meat wasn't left for the dead one. Maybe they all sat around the grave eating and threw in a bone."

"You know, it really is hard to reconstruct beliefs on such scanty evidence."

"I'd like to make a guess about the position. That reminded me of the fetal position, and maybe they thought of death as a return to the womb and thought of the earth as the mother. So this was returning the dead to the womb of the great mother earth."

"Wow."

"But if bodies get stiff after death, the others would have to cram it in in that position right away, before it stiffened."

"So that could easily have become a custom, to put them in that position."

"Maybe they tied the body in that tight position. It doesn't seem very restful to me curled up that tight."

"You know, the afterlife isn't always thought of as benevolent and happy. Maybe the family was afraid of the spirits of the dead and actually tied them into this position so that they couldn't walk around and bother the living anymore."

"It's like the difference between angels and ghosts. We think of one as good and the other as bad or scary. They could have been scared of the ghosts of the dead. Afterlife can mean lots of things."

"Let's get down to the most basic items. This definitely is a grave where he was buried. So the survivors had to have dug it and placed the body there. The tools show that some sort of ceremony took place. But why bury at all? That is a lot of work. Why not toss the body out for the animals to finish? Once more, it looks like a tradition that these people had carried on. Are there any more graves like this one? Are they nearby?"

Teacher: "There are more graves, but let's consider this one a little more."

"That notion of the fetal position and returning to the womb sounds fanciful to me, and I guess it is because of the rule we used earlier about taking the explanation with the fewest assumptions. What was that called?"

"Occam's razor."

"Yeah, Occam's razor. Use the simplest explanation and you'll probably be right."

"It's also called the law of parsimony."

"If we're going to follow the simplest explanation, then I can dispose of Happy Hunting Grounds and wombs and ghosts. Just assume that it was winter, the ground was frozen, and these guys got tired of digging a big hole, so they crammed the body into a small hole."

"Hey, that's really simple. You really are parsimonious as well as plain stingy. We could call it the Theory of the Lazy Gravediggers."

"Maybe that also explains why the grave is in a cave. Maybe in the summer they buried them outside and in the winter they buried them near the fire, where the ground was not so hard."

"But still, they did dig a grave to bury their dead. And that seems to indicate a caring for a member of the group. They did leave things in the grave, and that indicates some beliefs about either the afterlife or that no one wanted to use a dead man's weapons."

Teacher: "Well, you have come up with some pretty interesting theories and speculations that fit the facts. What more would you need to know in order to settle on a certain theory?"

"We would need more evidence, more digs."

"We would need another dig near this one and at the same time level, I mean the same age. Then we might be dealing with the same culture and the same time period. And if they all had tools and food in them, that would support some sort of afterlife."

"And if they were all buried lying on the right side, that would certainly indicate a tradition or a custom as well."

Teacher: "Pretty soon we shall get to more evidence, and then you can check some of your speculations against additional evidence."

*   *   *

I was the teacher in many classes like that, and they were fun.

The notion of inquiry teaching is that you give those big-brained students of yours a chance to use their big brains. Just because some writer has said that burials indicate a belief in after-life, that does not preclude students from coming up with a whole set of variations. Telling them in advance cuts off that chance. Don't tell them; let them speculate and astonish themselves and, probably, astonish you too.

Also notice the testing of ideas. The group will speculate, will make all sorts of wild inferences, but will stay tethered to the facts in front of them. Nobody disproved the return-to-the womb notion, but the law of parsimony made it seem less tenable. And the law of parsimony can be challenged as well.

An hour could easily be spent on listing the kinds of evidence that they would want in addition. New digs give us more evidence, but seldom just what we would wish for.

You have just seen the basic formula for inquiry teaching: Give students a set of facts and slip the leash. They speculate, they create new concepts, they apply old concepts, they test, they reject, they ask for more evidence. And the more of this process you can have students verbalize, the more conscious students will become of the way they are learning to infer, to test, to reject, to accept, and to help each other learn.

Cooperation is also a good thing to learn.

*   *   *

One brief note on honesty in reporting. No class of students who are groping for ideas and ways to express them would be as glib as this gang appears to be. Normal conversation is filled with "aaah, and-uh, hey, how about, aaah, you know, basically, like, and-uh, maybe, could be, you know, aah, like I said, basically, you know, and-uh," plus all the tedious and unmelodic gurgling noises we make when thinking out loud and trying to get a word edgewise into a group's cooperative activity. No, I did not tape-record my classes. Many times I did make notes later. These reports are based on those notes.

In the interest of readability, such noises are edited out. You are welcome.

One more point. I have no nephew named Jack who teaches history. Jack is a fiction, an artifact. When my wife read his pretentious style, turgid with polysyllables and stuffed with semicolons, always struggling to achieve a periodic sentence, she commented: "He writes the way you did in college." Jack just might be my much younger self striving to appear the polymath. But the letters bearing my name show a fairly accurate account of my early teaching.

*　　*　　*

A seventy-year-old Chippewa Indian gave me an unforgettable lesson in learning by observation.

At the Red Lake Indian Reservation in northern Minnesota, I was busy one summer studying elderly Indians. One of my tools was taking down family trees using the Chippewa words and names.

To do this, I would carry in a big piece of rolled up brown wrapping paper to draw on while asking questions. As I got the answers, I sketched in mother and father and sisters and brothers and all their names and nicknames and relationship terms. Actually, I did not know how to speak Chippewa, which is an enormously complex language; what I knew was how to write down the sounds phonetically so that I could return and pronounce them correctly the next day or the next week.

Ray Cloud could not speak English. He was about seventy then, a grizzled old fisherman living at Ponemah in his little house wrapped with tar paper to keep out the wind. He was courteous and smiled and listened carefully as Tom Cain interpreted for me. He would answer and repeat if I needed it, which I frequently did.

So there the three of us were. Ray sat on his bed. Tom sat on the chair. I sat on a big overturned wooden fish box with my brown wrapping paper, writing out my chart. The sun shone through the open door and the window. Two wood stoves, one bed, and one table filled up most of the rest of the one room. I had got two generations back and was tracing some collaterals when Ray pointed at the chart and said something in Chippewa.

"Ray says you got that chart wrong," said Tom.

The old man had been watching me draw circles for women and triangles for men and lines linking them. For him, the chart was upside down, and he could not read my writing—or any writing, for that matter.

Ray bent over and traced out the correction with his finger. I had linked a brother where I should have shown a cousin. Just by watching me, Ray had learned the whole kinship system as I drew it. He had figured out my symbols for male and female and my vertical lines for descent and my horizontal lines for siblings and my equals signs for marriage.

Now, there was a bright student. Without knowing English, without knowing how to read or write, and looking at my chart upside down, he had learned my system well enough to correct my error. He observed, and he used his big brain. He saw me translate his answers into symbols and quickly grasped the conventions of drawing a family tree: the gender symbols, the descent symbols, the marriage symbols, the sibling symbols.

Ray taught me how to teach that morning. He taught me how to teach my college students the conventions of sketching a family tree. Don't tell them; show them. Let them figure it out, and they will remember it longer and have the fun of doing it. After they have done it, you can pass out a handout summarizing the rules that they have doped out by themselves. After, not before.

Long after I met Ray, I met a white woman teacher who referred to Indians as "stupid Indians." I shall get back to her later.

My point here is that human beings love puzzles, and most students turn out to be very human if given a chance. They are much like teachers, most of whom also turn out to be human.

The problem or puzzle approach solves immediately the inattention of students who might prefer to daydream or to write a letter or to play footsie or to study for a test in another class, a preference that Chet Meyers noticed in so many classes when he wrote, "Where is that childlike sense of wonder, inquisitiveness, and playfulness in a group of passive college students, almost daring a teacher to spark their interest in philosophy or literature? Shouldn't we expect at least as much interest from students as chimpanzees exhibit?" (Meyers, 1986, p. 41).

When I learned to use a transparency on an overhead projector with the room lights off, the students couldn't see to read other books anyway. Captives.

*   *   *

Dr. Gray took the six of us for a walk in the woods. Suddenly he squatted down, staring at a plant. We all hunkered down around the plant, guessing names, showing off our knowledge.

Dr. Gray ignored our chatter. He asked one fellow to describe the leaves.

"Four leaves. Oval shaped. All at the top of the stem."

"Do they all have four leaves?"

Quickly we began looking for other plants. We were standing on them. "This one has six." "Here's four." "This one has five." "Another four."

"Okay. Now you, you describe the flower." He pointed at me.

"White petals. Four white petals. Small."

"Do they all have four white petals?"

Again we all hastily checked. They all had four white petals.

"All right. Now the stem." He pointed to another.

"About six inches. Round. Smooth. All the leaves branch out at the top, and so does the flower."

"Okay again. Now this plant develops berries in the fall. Who knows what color they are?"

Silence. One spoke up. "Red, bright red. A bunch of them."

Dr. Gray smiled. "And I think that you also know the name."

"Bunchberry," grinning proudly.

"Good. Now you describe the bunchberry once more for all of us."

"It has one stem about six inches high. Out of that come four or five or more oval leaves. Out of the center of the leaves comes the flower, with four white petals. That develops into a bunch of red berries."

Dr. Gray rose to his feet. "Excellent. Now you all know the bunchberry and what it looks like."

We walked on, hunkering down again to describe in detail a trillium, a wild onion, then an anemone.

He stopped once by some small plants with four leaves and white flowers. It was the one we had first examined. I could even see the bunch of red berries coming in the fall. We all hesitated and then blurted out almost together, "Bunchberry."

Then he showed us a new one, then one we had already learned. Then more new ones, with repeats of the old for review. Never did he tell us we were right or wrong in guessing at names. He just waited until we had looked carefully at the plant, the stem, the leaves, the flowers, the seeds. And he waited until we had described each in words. Once he pulled a tiny plant out by the roots to show us the gold root that gave it its name. Then he replanted it, pressing the soil with strong fingers.

We were all teaching nature at the Chicago Boy Scout Camps near Muskegon, Michigan, that long-ago summer of 1936. This was a special training session for two naturalists from each of three camps, designed to teach the teachers something about all those green things that grow on the forest floor. Like me, the rest knew birds and trees and snakes and turtles and small animals and stars, at least enough to teach twelve-year-olds. None of us knew much about those little green things that you walk on.

For several hours we walked and squatted. We learned the new and reviewed the old. We practiced. We observed. We described. We reviewed.

He also taught us something more valuable than the names and descriptions of small plants. He taught us how to teach others.

Once he pointed to a plant as we walked by. "That's bone-set." We all walked on. He stopped and pointed at me. "Describe boneset."

"I didn't even look at it."

"Let's go look at it." Back we trooped to give boneset the full treatment. Now we noticed how the opposite leaves had grown together in such a way that the stem seemed to pierce one big leaf.

"Why didn't you look at the leaf before?"

"Because we were mostly eager to know the name. Once we heard the name, we quit thinking."

It was a very valuable lesson. All that summer, working with groups of twelve- and thirteen-year-old scouts, I used the same method as much as I could. Hold back the name until they have observed and described. Observations first. Descriptions first. Most of us quit thinking once we get the label. So hold back on the label. First make people look, see, describe.

And Dr. Gray never nagged, never criticized, never told us we were wrong or lazy or weren't paying attention. He got us interested, and he worked us through his method. Look, see, describe, and finally get the label.

Years later, I observed the utter negation of this method. An enthusiastic birdwatcher took a group out for a walk on an island in northern Minnesota.

"There's a nuthatch. Can you hear it? And there's a red-winged blackbird in the swamp. And I hear a red-eyed vireo. And that bird flies like a goldfinch."

She chatted on and on and on. The poor dear was so intent upon showing us how much she knew that nobody had a chance to settle on one bird long enough to look, to see, and to describe. She labeled everything and taught nothing.

Dr. Gray became my role model. I tried to imitate his methods. Look carefully, describe, and label at the last.

The birder was an anti-role model, the sort of person your mother warned about, "Don't be like that."

As for the labeling, we have all seen that desire to label in the political arena. Affix the label and never mind listening or observing the facts.

And there is some decent learning theory behind this, as Jean Piaget observed in children between six and eleven when they begin to generalize and to categorize. At this stage, they relate directly to the visible world, the touchable world. They like names. Abstractions come later, when they are older (Johnson, 1981, p. 42).

Which leads us to the point that Chet Meyers makes: "The

key . . . is the order of movement: concrete experience first, then abstraction. This idea may seem like mere common sense—but it stands in direct opposition to traditional teaching methods which introduce abstractions through some concrete method of verification" (Meyers, 1986, p. 29).

Sherlock Holmes first studied facts to create his general rules, which he then applied to specific cases. He noticed that a dog barked at strangers but never at his master. Thus, when the dog did not bark at night, Holmes suspected that the master was the intruder.

In that same passage above, Meyers points out that science labs usually give theory first, with the lab as confirmation, not discovery. Most of us tell students and then use some facts to confirm what we told them. We don't let them discover. We don't let them have the fun. And then we complain that they seem bored.

*   *   *

Our physics teacher, Bill Walton, was forever constructing experiments. His classes often would measure circles for their diameter and their circumference and then divide to establish the value of pi. When a student said that he had memorized pi to seventeen places, Bill would grin, give him a tin plate, and say "Show me."

Of course, their measurements were sloppy and their instruments crude. Pie tins, wagon wheels, anything circular they measured to determine pi. As they worked, they improved in measuring skills and slowly got closer to the number they had all accepted on authority and faith.

Bill began with data. He had students measure and observe and then think it out. Facts first.

*   *   *

Now you have the basic formula: Present students with some cluster of facts and let them do the thinking. Most of us want to tell; we want to show off that we know; we want to appear smart.

But our job as teachers is not to preen our egos, even though preening is fun, but to prepare students to solve problems when we are no longer around. For some of us, that means that we teachers also have to learn to solve problems instead of memorizing answers. And that is because nobody trusted enough in our big brains to let us learn those skills of solving problems.

The actual teaching technique will vary with the discipline. History, physics, and botany will all handle different sorts of data. Yet the major approach is similar. Give them the material; let them decide what to do with it; and let them speculate on what generalization or label or abstraction best fits. The laboratory classes of the natural sciences could be superb at that, unless students are told what the result ought to be and then fudge the data to reach the result. I mean open-ended experiments, accepting answers within a range.

As for learning how the old professional handles the material, that should be visible in what the old pro has written. Look at a journal. The researcher describes all the previous material he has read; he describes the problem that is bothering him; he describes his new approach; he describes how he gathered his data; he describes his data and what they mean. The student can learn the protocol and the conventions and the rules through studying what has been published.

The students will be much happier. You will be much happier. You all will learn more. And you all will use those big brains more.

Now every researcher who has written a report in a journal knows that his or her polished final product is one far haul from the fumbling attempts and the sudden inspirations and the false starts of actual thinking and researching. Abraham Kaplan (1964) pointed out the difference in his description of thinking in his book on methodology for the behavioral sciences, which he titled *The Conduct of Inquiry*. There Kaplan distinguished between the logic of inquiry and the reconstructed logic-in-use afterward. The real groping and starting over are far different from the polished report written later.

If you devote one-fifth of your class time to inquiry teaching, you still can deliver those beautifully polished lectures on which you have spent so much loving attention. But something strange will happen, as you will learn later.

Try it one-fifth of your class time.

3

Some Insights from Piaget and Perry

Why bother with this kind of teaching by inquiry? Why not tell students what you are going to tell them, then tell them, and then tell them what you told them?

It worked for the rest of us, didn't it? The teachers laid it out clearly, told us to learn it, and gave a test, and then some of us moved on. And some of us had to study for a retest. We learned it. That is, we memorized it.

The assumption behind this traditional method is that the teacher knows something that is accurate and valuable and will be accurate next year. The student is ignorant. The teacher imparts this information, and the student learns it and becomes less ignorant.

The metaphor for this kind of education is the empty bucket. The teacher is the fountain of wisdom filling up all those empty buckets. The metaphor for knowledge is the water. It is clean, pure, drinkable, and worthwhile.

Well, maybe lots of what we teach fits that metaphor. Perhaps most. We do need fountains of wisdom or, anyway, fountains of knowledge.

Yet the stimulating teachers, the memorable teachers, are those who go beyond memorizing and teaching the same patterns over and over again. Somehow, they learned along the way that the best thing a teacher can do is to inspire students to learn on their own, to learn without the teacher. And the best thing they can do is to move students to the point where they can detect humbug, steer

27

away from phony advertising, detect errors in political speeches, get a feel for the fraudulent claims bombarding us, and even create new knowledge in scientific research. If they cannot actually commit research, they can understand the methods well enough to respect the nature of a tentative conclusion based on evidence as against the loud assertion of trust based on authority.

But I'm jumping ahead. Let's return to learning.

Psychologists know a lot about learning now. And much today depends on the work of a Swiss researcher named Jean Piaget.

Piaget, who carefully observed children playing and learning and developing concepts, considers his work to be epistemology rather than psychology. That word you can look up in the dictionary all by yourself. Whatever you call it, lots of us lean on Piaget.

Before I get in too deep, let me acknowledge where I got most of this educational theory. Right now I'm using a book by Eric W. Johnson (1981) called *Teaching School*. I'm also using a book by P. G. Richmond (1971) titled *An Introduction to Piaget*. Piaget himself has published many books; they are variously described as stimulating and provocative. They are also difficult to read and require intensely careful study. They do not lend themselves easily to summary quotations. So I suggest that you begin with a book like Richmond's. And I am also using the ideas expressed by Chet Meyers (1986) of Metropolitan College in Minneapolis in his book *Teaching Students to Think Critically*.

Now back to theory. Jean Piaget finds and describes several rather distinctive stages of learning in growing children.

In the first, infants learn to control their muscles to respond to their senses. Thumb-sucking, reaching, balancing, walking, picking up and letting go, and talking—all are sensorimotor skills usually learned before the age of two. Out of those skills, the child also learns a lot about the nature of rubber balls and wooden blocks and water and blankets and teddy bears and metal cups. The child learns which roll, which bounce, which make loud noises when pounded on the floor, which are soft and cuddly, and which can be sucked and chewed. The child is learning about the world out there and using every sense organ to help. The child is creating mental constructs for this world as the learning goes on.

The second stage, which usually lasts from about age two

until about age five, Piaget calls the period of prelogical thought. The child may imagine things and events and not distinguish clearly between real and imaginary events. But the child is not a passive recipient of data from the outside-the-skin world. No, the child interacts with that environment by creating mental patterns to organize that learning. These constructs have also been called blueprints and maps and designs and patterns. Nowadays, with so many people using computers, we might say that the construct is like a program that helps us to solve problems.

The stage that Piaget identifies as the third, the period of concrete operations, is a time of great learning. It is a time when we learn to look carefully at things, to count them, to organize them into categories and concepts, to remember and enjoy remembering, to be able to do operations inside our heads, to imagine "what if" situations, and still to keep real things distinct from "made-up" or imaginary things.

But the new learning comes at a cost. Many of the mental constructs of the very young child no longer work. Fantasy and magic no longer work. As the child reaches out more and more, the earliest road maps fail. The child rebuilds them because their use gets in the way, even though many of us still cling to fantasy and magic in daydreams.

This stage typically lasts from about five till about eleven or twelve years of age. But it can also last till fifteen or even fifty. Many never grow beyond it. In this stage, they learn rules of games in such a way that the rules become almost sacred.

But when they get to college, or high school, or even junior high school, we expect them to be entering the fourth stage of Piaget's scheme, the period of formal operations.

In our culture, this often comes about the time of adolescence, at about age twelve or thirteen. At this time, students learn to deal with abstractions and to know that they are abstractions, not real things. The students can understand systems of grammar and mathematics, can look at some evidence and construct a theory to explain the evidence, and then can construct a test to find out whether the theory works with new evidence. They learn that the rules of games can be modified by agreement. The future can be considered as something under partial control, because choices made today will affect life tomorrow.

Once again, the shift comes at a cost, for the learner must abandon those earlier mental blueprints that no longer work. Only a feeling of being off balance will force a learner to make these changes. Disequilibrium thus leads to growth. The discomfort of giving up simpler and more childish concepts leads to building more mature concepts. The learner is learning to think critically.

The ability to think critically and abstractly sometimes arrives early in precocious children, much to the amazement and wonder and consternation of their parents and teachers.

Thinking abstractly seems to be an essential human activity, and yet many of us never reach that fourth stage. Some persons are stuck in a preadolescent mental stage. Eric Johnson estimates that nearly half of all Americans never reach that stage of formal operations and dealing with abstractions. Many of us reach it only imperfectly and unevenly. We may be in the fourth stage for our professional lives yet still be stuck in the third stage for our other beliefs. Some of the zealots and fanatics that you meet appear to be stuck in that third stage. And some of the cynical manipulators of the public treat us all as if we were in that third stage.

Teachers must realize this, says Johnson. It is very important that teachers realize that some of their charges may never learn to think abstractly at all. They may never enter the fourth stage.

*   *   *

The disequilibrium mentioned above is a key to adult learning. Only when we fail to make sense of the world because we are applying the wrong blueprint will we grow by building new blueprints, new patterns for organizing learnings, new programs for our mental computer.

It is the teacher's job in inquiry teaching to provoke the disequilibrium. Then the student will want to change and will be able to build a new pattern, a new blueprint. But the student will be uncomfortable and will resist. The two processes go on almost together. As the student works with data and creates a new pattern, that same student may suddenly realize that all of his or her observations and logic are leading him or her to disavow and reject an old belief. It can be frightening.

As Meyers (1986, pp. 14-15) points out, "One reason that reconstructing thinking processes can be painful is that structures of thought are not merely matters of dispassionate cognition. They are also highly personal and emotional, involving cherished values and beliefs. . . . It can thus become a very emotion-laden process."

And again (p. 15), "One of the keys to teaching critical thinking successfully is to simultaneously challenge students' old modes of thinking and provide structure and support for the development of new ones."

This very strong emotional attachment to certain old blueprints or maps of the world makes new learning difficult.

If we have learned that our government can do no wrong and has never been wrong and has never broken a treaty or lied to another country or provoked a war, either we shall go through some pain in relearning history or we shall be stuck with a map that does not serve as a useful guide to the choices in adult life. The agony of adjusting to the reality of the Vietnam War shows both of these responses—the pain of readjustment and the stubborn refusal to admit errors. The civil rights struggle also illustrates these mental positions.

If we have learned that the Bible contains only great truths about loving each other and will serve as a guide to every decision in life, we will suffer great pain when we discover conflicting statements in the Bible, hear conflicting interpretations, or discover sectarian conflicts, or else we will cling to a stubborn refusal to admit such contradictions.

Those two areas of religion and nationalism probably provide the most emotionally charged blueprints or maps in our lives. Thus, the victim of incest who represses the memory of a brutal parent for years because of the commandment to "Honor thy father and mother" is cruelly trapped. Many such victims live their lives in torment until they can unburden themselves to a therapist. Part of the therapist's job is to assist the client to reexamine old mental constructs and build new and more realistic ones.

The therapist cannot just tell the client what to do. The therapist can only help such suffering clients to examine their old patterns until they are ready to reject and build anew. It can be a painful process.

As Carl Westphal taught us when he was training peer counselors in an Elder Network program, if old habits bring you pain, you must change your old habits.

> "If you keep on doing what you've always done,
> you'll keep on getting what you've always got."

*   *   *

What I have called inquiry teaching is sometimes called inductive teaching or discovery teaching.

And it is tightly overlapped with what we call teaching critical thinking.

The main similarity seems to be that both systems ask the student to look afresh at data, to look first at the data without realizing that blueprints exist, and to construct new blueprints, new maps, without dependence on the old constructs.

Most of the students' new constructions turn out to be very similar to the teacher's old and functioning blueprints. When we reinvent the wheel, it looks much like the old wheel. A very few of these invented constructs might turn out to be exciting and refreshingly new, delightful glimpses through a new lens. In such a case, the teacher must be willing to consider a daring and bold way to perceive created by a student. Some of our students will make a quantum leap far ahead of us. And that can be wrenching for teachers, just as it is for students. We must remember to remain students forever, willing to learn.

*   *   *

Chet Meyers also summarizes some work of Robert Karplus, former dean of the graduate school at Berkeley. Karplus used the theory of Piaget and applied it to children and then found it so effective that he used it in college teaching with great effectiveness (Meyers, 1986, pp. 31-34).

Karplus used a three-stage learning cycle. First, students explore the materials already selected as valuable by the teacher. They probe and wonder and brainstorm and query and find that some of the data upset their earlier blueprints.

The teacher helps but does not lecture or provide answers. The teacher encourages. The teacher creates an attitude of permission. "The most important aspect of this part of the learning cycle is the creation of an atmosphere in which probing, puzzling, and raising questions provide a natural challenge to the students' present mental structures, thereby creating the disequilibrium necessary for change" (p. 32).

In the second stage, the students invent concepts, generalizations, or principles in an attempt to garner some meaning out of the materials—they build abstractions. "This part of the learning cycle is usually the most challenging and frustrating to teachers. They must not rush to draw conclusions for students, but rather let students struggle with the trial and error and the discomfort involved in developing new ways of thinking" (p. 32).

In the final stage, students use the principles or concepts that they invented and apply them to other material as a test of their validity. A successful test is a stunning reinforcement. That kind of learning you never forget.

The hardest part for me as a teacher was to keep my mouth shut. No lectures. No shortcuts. Let the students puzzle and wonder and find for themselves that their old blueprints no longer fit. Let them help each other. Let them persuade each other. The roads on the old map do not follow the design of the roads in the real world. As teacher, you may not have the fun of delivering that brilliant lecture, but you do have the fun of being midwife to a new idea, a new concept, a new generalization that a student will cherish forever.

*   *   *

April 16, 1989

Dear Walter,

Your manuscript was delightful to read, even though you obviously used methods far different from mine.

Therefore, to criticize is going to be difficult, so I shall simply plunge in and say what comes to mind in regard to two basic items. First, I am quite reluctant to have students speculate about data without some instant correction. They can froth all over guessing what did happen or may happen or should happen or will happen. And unless they get a bucket of cold facts thrown on their fancy speculations, they will remember their guesses and not realize that history did not happen that way. That struck me as a waste of valuable class time. Better that they learn the facts. They are paying to learn the truth, not to collect speculations.

One supervisor impressed on me: Never let a class leave the room with incorrect ideas in mind.

As for the theories of Piaget, I hesitate again to engage in ultracrepidarian criticism, being an utter stranger to his theories. However, I fail to see how studying child psychology is going to help me teach history. My youngest students are 19 or 20 years old and should be mature by now; if they are not, that is their problem, and hardly one to be cured in a history class.

Aside from that, you do have some delightful stories. They were fun to read even though I seem to disagree with your basic premises. Maybe there are many good ways to teach, depending on the time and the place and the personality. Please send me more. Also, I checked a few typos such as "goal" with two g's.

Historically and critically,

Jack

*   *   *

Another book on inquiry teaching made quite a splash several years ago. Neil Postman and Charles Weingartner (1969) wrote a delightfully angry book with a title that grabbed you: *Teaching as a Subversive Activity*. Lots of people read it with delight and excitement.

Postman and Weingartner leaned heavily on theory used by the semanticists, writers such as S. I. Hayakawa, who made the theories of Alfred Korzybski understandable to millions.

They took a dim view of the traditional classroom, writing that it was rigid and authoritarian and did all the wrong things. When you think of the worst teacher you ever had, you get a glimpse of what Postman and Weingartner were describing. They described classrooms where students were:

> Accepting passively instead of thinking critically
> Memorizing instead of solving problems
> Never encouraged to discover knowledge

The teachers in these classrooms

> Taught students to trust in authority: the teacher, the text, the principal
> Did not consider student feelings as important
> Believed that each question has a single right answer

Their final summation of a rigid curriculum deserves quoting in full: "English is not History and History is not Science and Science is not Art and Art is not Music, and Art and Music are minor subjects and English, History, and Science major subjects, and a subject is something you 'take' and, when you have taken it, you have 'had' it, and if you have 'had' it, you are immune and need not take it again" (pp. 20-21).

The strongest recommendation that Postman and Weingartner make is to encourage students to ask questions. Most questions in a classroom are asked by the teacher, and most of them demand a simple recall of a single word. Memory is stressed. But Postman and Weingartner want students to ask questions and then to spend some time figuring out the answers to what they think is important.

What they advocate is a lot like the approach of inquiry

described here. Give the students some data and let them come up with queries. Let them answer their own questions and then either give them more data or have them hunt up their own. Then they gradually construct mental blueprints that fit. They may invent lots of them. Some may sound pretty wild, but the other students will tame them down and smooth off the rough edges and persuade each other.

Questions. Questions are the key to good teaching, and the student must have some interest in the question as a reasonable way to attack a body of puzzling data. And it is questions that Chet Meyers suggests as a way to make that shift into using a few inquiry techniques. Confirmed and competent lecturers may find that beginning a class with a general question or a problem will prepare students for discussion and for thinking instead of just taking notes or daydreaming or worrying about their job or their date or their husband or their income.

If you wish to test the waters of inquiry teaching before plunging in completely, try posing a question before a good lecture.

Then give the students time to think. Time. And that means accepting silence.

First they will throw it back at you. Smile and wait. Finally, someone will come up with a tentative answer.

If you agree, do not say so. No. Never. Just smile.

Turn to another student and ask, "Do you agree with that?" Whatever response you get, keep on throwing it back until someone starts supporting a position with facts and argument. Then the question is getting sharpened, and they begin to see that it is a question of importance. Urge them to develop several tentative answers.

After that you can lecture. This time, more of them may take notes. If the discussion took up some precious lecture time, be comforted. They were thinking. And that is really the ultimate goal of a good teacher.

The next time you begin with a question, ask the students to huddle in groups of three or four. Not only will you involve almost every person in the room, you will also send the clear message that you consider their thinking important. Just remember that thinking takes some time and some silence. It also shows the teacher's respect for the student.

*   *   *

So far, we've been stressing Piaget's fourth stage of formal operations, in which the young student learns to examine new data and to recast his or her old mental patterns into more successful mental patterns.

A group of teachers at Harvard, while attempting to help bright young freshmen learn to study, and learn to learn, and learn to construct new patterns of thought, took the time to analyze the growth process into stages. The scheme of nine stages that they described is now usually referred to as "the Perry Scheme" (Perry, 1970). It could be considered as an expanded version of Piaget's fourth stage, a nine-rung ladder on which the student climbs from stage three to stage four.

The climbing is the interesting part, the transition from one rung to the next. As you read this list of mental positions, think of them as a series of blueprints that work for a time until they are replaced with ones that work better. (I translated the original wording into my own.) Each stage or position or rung is numbered. The transitions, in italics, reveal the growth and change.

1. Things are either Right or Wrong, Good or Bad, In-Group or Out-Group. Good Students must work hard to learn the Right Answers. Teachers already know the Right Answers.

Growth comes from realizing that the right answers occasionally disagree and that opinions differ. With growth, the student moves to the next position.

2. The Right Answers come from the True Authorities, so stick with them. Avoid False Authorities, who are bad.

Further growth comes from realizing that even True Authorities may give tentative answers. Some things they don't know yet.

3. So don't be upset if you have some uncertainties, because the True Authorities are researching right now to find the correct answer. Stay tuned. Soon they will tell you.

The Perry scheme lumps these first three stages under the rubric of Dualism, a simple polarity of two values with the student slowly questioning its simplicity. For an exercise in familiarizing myself with these positions, I have been reading letters to the editor in the newspaper and attempting to match the letter writers' thought processes with Perry's stages. You also may find this instructive, as well as entertaining. But I must be wary, for my classifications also depend on what position I have reached. We can reach different levels in regard to different parts of our life.

The growth out of Dualism leads to a general position of Multiplicity. And that requires more growth, stemming from the awareness that even the True Authorities don't know the answers.

4a. And if they don't know the answers, then my opinion is as good as theirs. No one is wrong. What counts is the context. (Many students get permanently stuck with this fake relativistic stance: If no one knows, then anything goes.)

But how can instructors grade us if no one can be proved wrong?

4b. (alternate position). Maybe it's grading based on how well we can think and argue and organize facts in support of their position.

But that sort of thinking is valuable outside of class as well. Everywhere.

5. Then it is clear thinking that we are searching for. Opinions may be good in one context, but not all are going to stand up to criticism. These different theories are just handles for understanding data.

In a world where all is relative, how can I make the Correct Choice?

6. If no one can ultimately tell me, then it looks as though I must make my own decisions as best I can. Just believing in teachers or books is not enough.

Maybe that first choice is crucial. Once I choose my career, all the rest will fall into place. That will be my first Commitment.

7. There. My career choice is made. All is well. I am Committed. All the rest will now fall into place.

But how come I still have more problems and choices?

8. Are all my choices dependent on other choices? Is my whole life to be tentative? How can I live with eternal contingency? How can I cope with an eternal "if"?

Life is getting more complex and contradictory and contingent the more I learn and choose.

9. Yes, life is tentative. Choices are tentative. Positions are

tentative. Even those beliefs that I cherish the most I must be ready to modify if I learn data that contradict them. But until I change those values, I can work firmly with the best answers I have today. I have made Commitments, made choices, and I can defend them. Yet I can also respect the choices of others.

Positions 6 through 9 come under the heading of Commitment, meaning that the student, aware of the relative and tentative nature of knowledge, has still made a conscious choice. And that student has made it on his or her own, not by indoctrination or emotional conversion.

Perry's long safari from sheer Dualism into Multiplicity and then into Relativism to reach conscious Commitment provides a series of glimpses into the reconstructing of mental blueprints. It also gives a glimpse of the discomfort of growth and the pain of relinquishing long-held views.

Look back at some of Jack's letters in Chapter One. Where would you place them on the Perry rungs?

Our students enter college at many levels on this scheme. Listen to Laurent Daloz (1987, p. 81) in *Effective Teaching and Mentoring:* "My own research (1981) suggests that most adults returning to college arrive carrying some degree of dualism and a good deal of multiplicity. That is, they are moving away from exclusive reliance on external authority as the source of 'truth,' toward skepticism of such authority (albeit sometimes rather dualistic skepticism) and the belief that any opinion is as good as any other. This is when the journey gets exciting, for it is during this time as the old foundations begin to crumble that the footings are laid for the transformation that Perry describes as the 4/5 transition, the central transformation of his scheme and very probably of a good college education."

*   *   *

As we learn "facts" about a subject, we also learn how those facts were gathered and tested. We learn that some are still argued about and some are barely tentative. The student who is trying to comprehend a body of knowledge should also realize that the techniques of the professional who does the research are also very important. The student should early on be exposed to the methods of research and the methods of proof. Not that every student will become a researcher, but knowing how knowledge is gathered will make one more willing to assume a tentative position. We can be less dogmatic. We can realize that we might even change our minds.

The teacher who uses inquiry expects students to learn lots of facts. While learning those facts, the students can also learn methods, learn criticism, and learn the tentative quality of decisions and the spread between untested speculations and theories that have long held up under testing.

That mature level of acceptance that your life can be faced with confidence tempered with the reservation that tomorrow you might just change your conclusion if someone can provide new evidence is not for everyone. The attitude that your life can be supported by deep values while you are still ready to learn more will never be wildly popular.

Many of us cannot face a fully rational and scientific attitude of believing that we are right yet admitting that all beliefs are tentative in some way. Perhaps more of us could if only we started at an earlier age. It is the ultimate freedom, and those who cannot accept the painful decisions of freedom are legion. Seeking authority is the common escape from the fear of freedom. A society that strives to be democratic needs many citizens who need not escape because they do not fear freedom.

*   *   *

Should you feel, as Jack did, that students should not leave any classroom with the wrong ideas, consider what a burden of bias each carried into that classroom. Facing all that, you may never let your people go.

Let us take a look at bias. *Bias* is another name for those early patterns of thinking. It is also the name for the later patterns of thinking, although those ought to be more congruent with the world.

QUESTION TWO

HOW CAN YOU
TEACH BY INQUIRY?

Chapters Four through Thirteen present illustrative examples of the uses of inquiry and discovery in the classroom while teaching a variety of topics. Using inquiry and discovery, you will engage the students' interest, raise their critical abilities, focus their learning, and provide subject matter of sufficient importance to help them build new mental patterns while discarding some old assumptions.

4

Discovering
Your Own Bias

The class of nursing students was discussing a chapter on inherited race differences, and the teacher was struggling to make the point that none were significant to behavior. I was not doing very well.

One young woman told about a church convention in her hometown in Iowa. The year was 1950. Ministers were housed with church families, and her married sister had been hosting a black minister.

"He slept in that bed for three nights. And when he left, the sheets were all black. My sister had a hard time washing them clean."

My face betrayed me. Another student asked, "Don't you believe that?"

"Well, skin color doesn't rub off. The color isn't even on the surface of the skin, it is . . . "

"Are you calling my sister a liar?" The first student cried out angrily. She had abruptly shifted the question from the flakiness of skin to the flakiness of her sister.

"No, I don't know your sister. But this is a question that can easily be solved by observing. How many of you have dealt with black patients in the hospital?"

About half of the class indicated that they had.

"Well, let's look. I want all of you to check on those patients and check the sheets and see for yourself whether black skin rubs off on the sheets."

"Are you calling my sister a liar?" She was almost screaming now. Two other students tried to calm her.

That was not the best intellectual climate for calm discussion. Somehow we got through the class.

Two days later, the class met again. Just before I walked in, three students stopped me in the hall.

"Please don't bring up that skin color problem. Poor Jane has had an awful two days. Everybody has been riding her. We all know very well that she was utterly wrong, and we kept inviting her into a hospital room to check on the sheets. She gets madder and madder. She knows she's wrong, but she can be so pigheaded."

"A couple of us even told her that if the sheets were dirty, it meant that some nurse hadn't bathed the patient."

We went in to discuss adolescence in Samoa.

Whether Jane learned much I don't know. But the thirty-nine other students all observed the data, discussed the data, and concluded that one common racial belief was pure nonsense. They did this by looking at dark-skinned patients lying on white sheets and thus convincing themselves. Those two days outside of class were filled with learning, with discovery learning based on focused observation.

Later, the same three talked to me again. "You know, I was ready to believe what Jane said. I never questioned some of that stuff; it was something we grew up believing. But when we spent two days looking deliberately at black patients on white sheets, we suddenly saw for the first time that it wasn't true. It simply wasn't true."

Another said, "It's sort of a shock to hear people say things that directly contradict their own eyes. But I guess that is what stereotypes and bias are all about."

*   *   *

Bias is so pervasive that knocking one myth on the head seldom has much influence on a thousand others. Yet we try.

Ethnocentrism is the deep-rooted foundation for many of our other biases. We think that our ways are better than the ways of anyone else. Our religion is right. Our country is the best. Our economic system is the only sensible way. Our political system is superb.

Some of those beliefs can be seriously defended. Other peoples do wish to immigrate here. Others do wish to emulate us. We do have a pretty good thing going.

But some side effects of snobbery, elitism, prejudice, discrimination, and a social system that systematically keeps many people out of school or doing stoop labor can be a high price to pay for a blind love affair with ourselves.

The common garden variety of ethnocentrism flourishes untended in all our minds. Teachers often use Ralph Linton's famous "100 percent American" passage in an attempt at weeding.

> Our solid American citizen awakens in a bed built on a pattern which originated in the Near East but which was modified in Northern Europe before it was transmitted to America. He throws back the covers made from cotton, domesticated in India, or linen, domesticated in the Near East, or wool from sheep, also domesticated in the Near East, or silk, the use of which was discovered in China. All of these materials have been spun and woven by processes invented in the Near East. He slips into his moccasins, invented by the Indians of the Eastern woodlands, and goes to the bathroom, whose fixtures are a mixture of European and American invention, both of recent date. He takes off his pajamas, a garment invented in India, and washes with soap invented by the ancient Gauls. He then shaves, a masochistic rite which seems to have been derived from either Sumer or ancient Egypt.
>
> Returning to the bedroom, he removes his clothes from a chair of southern European type and proceeds to dress. He puts on garments whose form originally derived from the skin clothing of the nomads of the Asiatic steppes, puts on shoes made from skins tanned by a process invented in ancient Egypt and cut to a pattern derived from the classical civilizations of the Mediterranean, and ties around his neck

a strip of bright-colored cloth which is a vestigial survival of the shoulder shawls worn by the seventeenth-
century Croatians. Before going out for breakfast he
glances through the window, made of glass invented
in Egypt, and if it is raining, puts on overshoes made
of rubber discovered by the Central American Indians
and takes an umbrella, invented in southeastern Asia.
Upon his head he puts a hat made of felt, a material
invented in the Asiatic steppes.

On his way to breakfast he stops to buy a paper,
paying for it with coins, an ancient Lydian invention.
At the restaurant a whole new series of borrowed elements confronts him. His plate is made of a form of
pottery invented in China. His knife is of steel, an alloy
first made in southern India, his fork a medieval Italian invention, and his spoon a derivative of a Roman
original. He begins breakfast with an orange, from the
eastern Mediterranean, a cantaloupe from Persia, or
perhaps a piece of African watermelon. With this he
has coffee, an Abyssinian plant, with cream and sugar.
Both the domestication of cows and the idea of milking
them originated in the Near East, while sugar was first
made in India. After his fruit and coffee he goes on to
waffles, cakes made by a Scandinavian technique from
wheat domesticated in Asia Minor. Over these he pours
maple syrup, invented by the Indians of the Eastern
woodlands. As a side dish he may have the eggs of a
species of bird domesticated in Indo-China, or thin
strips of the flesh of an animal domesticated in Eastern
Asia which have been salted and smoked by a process
developed in northern Europe.

When our friend has finished eating, he settles
back to smoke, an American Indian habit, consuming
a plant domesticated in Brazil in either a pipe, derived
from the Indians of Virginia, or a cigarette derived
from Mexico. If he is hardy enough he may even attempt a cigar, transmitted to us from the Antilles by
way of Spain. While smoking he reads the news of the

day, imprinted in characters invented in Germany. As
he absorbs the accounts of foreign troubles he will, if
he is a good conservative citizen, thank a Hebrew deity
in an Indo-European language that he is 100 per cent
American [Linton, 1936, pp. 326–327].

By itself, that is just a humorous passage. However, discussed
in context, it becomes more effective. As usual, the problem is that
most Americans know very little of their own history and none of
the history of other peoples. Because we are ethnocentric, we cannot
challenge ethnocentrism. And because others are also ethnocentric,
that somehow seems to make it even. It doesn't.

Travel is one answer. Travel to another country, learn the
language, learn the customs, study the religion, learn to enjoy the
food, wear the clothing. And thus you will conquer ethnocentrism.
Sure. Easy. Nothing to it.

Except that when most Americans travel, we insulate ourselves from the other culture. We photograph the Coliseum in
Rome, but we cannot speak Italian. We photograph Lenin's tomb,
but we do not speak Russian. We photograph the Great Wall, but
we do not talk with the Chinese unless they have learned to speak
English. And somehow the tourist industry manages to build Hil-
ton hotels all over the world, which provide us with the same amen-
ities that we are accustomed to.

Join the Peace Corps. Live like a native and speak the language and work with the locals. You will get over your culture
shock and get over a lot of ethnocentrism, and when you come home
you will run into the experience of culture shock for the second
time. Those who have done it have been changed forever. If you
can't do that, invite a returned P. C. volunteer in to talk to the class.

Reading is another way. At least it helps in minor ways.

The ideal method is to learn another culture so well that you
can admire it and like it and appreciate the values of that culture.
Then you can look back at your own culture to see it from an
outside perspective.

*　　　*　　　*

For years, my sociology students read a small novel by Hans Ruesch (1951) titled *Top of the World*. They read about a family of Polar Eskimos struggling to survive against the cold and the dangers in hunting seal or polar bears. They learned some of the customs and the strategies for survival among a hunting people whose way of life has not changed much since the Stone Age. And they learned to like the Eskimos and to giggle over some of their crude foods and cruder manners . . . as they seemed to the readers.

Then a white man enters the story, the kind that natives often meet first, a trader. This trader violates many of the customs of the Eskimos and also cheats them in trade, bartering worthless old muskets for hundreds of silver fox skins.

The students bristle at the insensitivity of an outsider who does not understand the culture of the Eskimos, as the students now think that they do. Later in the novel, a shouting missionary who tries to force his narrow brand of Christianity upon the natives raises the students' awareness even more. Each outsider is adamantly forcing his biased view of the world as an absolute truth that others must believe and follow.

The concept that they are learning about is ethnocentrism, the notion that my set of customs and beliefs are true and correct, and all others are false. It is a narrow view of the world, yet a very common one. Only by first taking the point of view of the Eskimo and thus resenting the bigotry of the intruder could my students gain a deep insight. They had to travel out, adopt another culture, in effect, and then observe how the white Americans behaved.

The result: insight. Suddenly they understood ethnocentrism and were irritated by the rude and self-righteous behavior of their own people. Many of them felt instantly superior to their ignorant brethren. They became biased in a different way.

The concept of ethnocentrism reappears. It comes back again and again, and each time students ought to gain a sharper knowledge and keener insight as to how one society looks at another.

Some are made so uncomfortable by this realization that they react with gasps of relief to the discovery that the Eskimos were also ethnocentric. "It's even, then. They think they are best, and we think we are best, so what difference does it make? We're even."

And from that point, we can introduce the concept of relative power to show the difference between a bigotry held by a large, powerful, and colonizing nation and that held by a tiny and power-less band of hunters.

Ethnocentrism persists as a problem for all of us. Students who read Dee Brown's (1970) account of our historical treatment of the American Indian in *Bury My Heart at Wounded Knee* brought hundreds of cases into class. But only those who read and discovered were really convinced. The others kept their old patterns. Yet those of us who gained insight had to gain insight over and over again. The values of our own culture are deep-rooted.

As they ought to be.

*   *   *

A history class would reach the Protestant Reformation. Their assignment included Luther's Ninety-Five Theses, that famous list of alleged abuses that Luther wanted scholars to debate and the church to correct.

The same question always arose: Was Luther right? Very quickly I learned to duck that question utterly. Let the class decide, or the individual. Use the library, bring back references by actual page. You tell us, and tell us why you think so.

I was weaning myself of the role of lecturer. Also, I was trying not to indoctrinate with my own views, particularly on a religious issue.

About one-third of my students were Catholics and about one-third were Lutherans. They were not particularly fond of each other, but most had learned to tolerate. Not all. The American notion of a pluralist society in which we maintain our own reli-gious values and at the same time respect the beliefs of others held a precarious footing in their minds and, as I learned, an even more precarious footing in some pulpits. The subject of the Reformation carried its own tension.

One student, Charlotte, said vehemently, "This whole Ninety-Five Theses stuff is a cover-up. Let's face it. Luther just got hot after a nun and wanted to break his vows."

Many gasped. A few of Charlotte's friends were nodding their heads in agreement. I took a plunge, not sure, but willing to risk it.

"I want you to bring in your documentation for that. In addition, I want you to look this up in the *Catholic Encyclopedia* or the *Britannica* and bring in dates and facts about Katherine von Bora."

"Who's she?"

And I gasped.

However, I refused to tell Charlotte. And I urged several other students to look up dates and facts about Katherine von Bora. I suggested the *Catholic Encyclopedia* because I had used it before and been impressed by its striving for historical accuracy rather than partisanship and thought that the Catholic students would accept it.

A few days later, the reports came in. Charlotte had looked up nothing except a religion textbook from her parochial high school. It did not support her statements; but she insisted that her teacher had told her about Luther and the nun.

Her friends were shocked. They had checked. They were shocked at her and at what they had discovered.

Katherine von Bora, they reported, had been raised largely by nuns and had taken the vows at the age of twelve. When Luther nailed his theses to the church door in 1517, Katherine was fourteen and in a convent. During the religious ferment in Germany in the following years, many monks and nuns left their orders. Katherine left in 1523, went to Wittenberg, and met Luther for the first time. They were married in 1525. They had six children and also raised eleven orphans.

Poor Charlotte never understood what all this discussion was about. She had certain blockages. When I met her father, I understood her a bit better.

*   *   *

The class reaction to Katherine was pale compared to the reactions when they looked up the histories of the Renaissance popes. This exercise I had started simply by answering a question with a question when they were reading passages from Machiavelli. "Who is this Cesare Borgia guy?"

"Who will be the first to find out and tell us?"

When they reported back that he was the son of Pope Alexander VI, the bulk of the class bridled in disbelief. So they checked on it themselves.

Score: Lutherans ahead on points. Catholics demoralized. A few days later, we were into the Peasant Wars in Germany and Luther's choice between the powerful rulers who supported him and the downtrodden peasants who were rebelling. He chose strength. In a famous letter entitled "Against the Murderous and Thieving Peasant Bands," he urged the princes of Germany to stab and strangle the peasant rebels. They did.

Catholics ahead on points. Lutherans demoralized. Then we reached the Council of Trent, the major workshop of the changes in the Catholic church. And when the class read the Proceedings of the Council of Trent and found that many of Luther's accusations about indulgences and illiterate priests who kept concubines were openly admitted by the church in an attempt to rectify the abuses, the class was finally ready to adopt a certain tolerance toward each other and each other's faith. Truth and virtue were not monopolies. Men and women in the past were just as fallible as we are today. The good old days were not always as good as they were old.

Discussions grew a bit more amiable. When one student rather smugly mocked both the Lutherans and the Catholics, I asked him what church he went to. He proudly replied: "Episcopalian."

"You shall have your day soon," I said. "And you will then understand why so many history teachers say, 'Thank God for Henry the Eighth.'"

Bias subtly bends our minds. It alters our perceptions, affecting what we see and hear and believe. And all we have learned so far in our lives alters our perceptions of what we can see. We cannot escape bias; it is the lens through which we see. However, we can realize our bias.

The bias written of here is the same as the patterns that Piaget writes of. Biases, or mental patterns, are the way in which we make sense of the world. Many of our mental patterns are learned whole from our parents and friends, untouched by facts.

Where would you place Charlotte on Perry's rungs? What is
the nature of her conflict?

*   *   *

About 1960, I received a small pamphlet from what was then
the Carnegie Institute of Technology in Pittsburgh and has now
become Carnegie-Mellon. It had only thirty-six pages. The title was
*Teaching the First Ten Assignments in an Introductory European
History Course*. It was written by a professor of history named Edwin Fenton.

This focused my ideas on teaching history. It was great. I had
found a clear description of a method that I found congenial.

Fenton's idea was similar to that of the composers of any
historical problems, a set of sources focused around a specific question. But Fenton was more helpful in his advice to the teacher. He
wanted young students to learn early on the skills of the historian,
the elementary methods of examining writers for their bias, their
reason for writing, their statements as to where they learned the
"facts" they were presenting, their separation of evidence and infer-
ence, their unconscious assumptions due to their having lived in a
particular place at a certain time.

That is quite an order for freshmen.

That is quite an order for students of any age.

But Fenton did not list for his classes all those intellectual
skills that he was planning to teach them. He just plunged in. He
gave them assignments that required certain judgments, and then the
class discussed those judgments. He did not tell them in advance.

Thus, he began with an assignment something like this: You
are writing a history of your own city in your own time. You have
three documents as sources. Of what value would each be?

1.   A description of your city written by a Mexican scholar after
     interviewing a number of Mexicans who had come as patients
     to the Mayo Clinic in Rochester.
2.   A history of the development of a labor union in the city writ-
     ten by its president twenty-three years later.

3.   An order from the mayor to the chief of police telling him how to deal with a group of "subversive agitators."

When I gave this assignment to my own class, the discussion usually took off instantly and then got blocked by an attempt to define words such as *city, in your own time,* and *history.* But those can be resolved. Few students even noticed that they should be careful with the words. Most just plunged in.

The discussion on the three documents might well reveal more of the bias of the class toward Mexicans, toward labor unions, and toward police than of the bias of the documents themselves. But it was really laying the foundation for the use of real documents to be read in the next few days, documents roughly comparable to the three just listed. The students learned to raise doubts as to reliability, doubts about the bias of a writer, doubts about the "official" bias of a legal report.

Then, still imitating Fenton, I assigned readings in a book on ancient Germany written by the Roman historian Tacitus. The students were to take notes on the possible answer to a specific question that I supplied. They were to take lots of notes and to identify whether those notes related to politics, economics, social organization, religion, and so on. With no shame at all, I assigned the question that Fenton had used: "What was the most important character trait of a German tribesman?"

The answer may not have been difficult; but the examination of the notes was the real goal. Students must learn to take notes for certain purposes and to be able to locate their sources in the reading when asked to. It's not easy, and most freshmen have never even tried to take such notes. They need practice. They need their notes checked for accuracy. They need more practice.

The class discussion, after a heavy session of checking on note-taking skills, would quickly settle on "courage" as the dominant character trait.

But there is more. Some of them noticed that Tacitus described all Germans as red-haired and blue-eyed. Had he ever been in Germany? A few other comments raise doubts as to his sources. Where did he get his facts? From merchants and returning soldiers? How much did they know? I used to ask veterans of the Korean War to describe the religious beliefs of Koreans to the class. They would snort in disgust. Many would reveal clearly not only the soldier's ignorance of the natives but his contempt for them. The class could see this, and, somewhat later, so could the veterans. During the Vietnam War, we used veterans of that conflict.

Then someone would suddenly catch on excitedly that this was comparable to the observations of the Mexican scholar writing about our city. Any writer is limited by his or her sources. What were the sources that Tacitus used? Tacitus does not tell us. But the class did suspect that he was not an eyewitness. He had never been to Germany, they were sure. They became wary of the sources used by a writer, especially when the writer does not reveal them to the reader.

And by learning to write careful notes, the students were learning to write.

*   *   *

Students wobble back and forth. They start out believing in the printed page. A few doubts make them instant skeptics who mistrust every printed page. They must learn some balance.

That balance comes with repeated exposures to the same basic questions: How well did the author tell you about her sources? How clearly did she separate her evidence from her inferences? How clearly did she reveal her attitude, her bias, toward the people that she was describing?

Now my basic belief in all this is that these critical skills are really the most important part of the history class. Yes, you should learn the narrative and have some notion of basic trends; but the thinking skills are what are most important.

Next, still following Edwin Fenton, I would expose the class to some basic information on Tacitus. It included his attitude toward the previous tyranny of the Emperor Domitian, his love of republican virtue, his love of the old-time Roman virtues of pride and courage and willingness to fight for one's own country instead of hiring mercenaries. Suddenly, they began to see why Tacitus was praising the Germans so much for their warlike behavior and their courage. He wanted Romans to act that way. He was setting up a model. He was writing with a purpose to persuade.

Students had already learned the bias of the source. Now they learned about the bias of the writer. They realized that in an age of hired writers, many will write what sells.

The third basic bias comes with a wallop. The assignment was to read part of the Acts of the Apostles, Luke's account of the earliest Christian community. The students were to compose two questions "that seem significant in the history of the early church and that do not require religious conviction or belief."

My students did reasonably well. But they ignored all of the skills that they had learned previously. They accepted the matter as written. They ignored contradictions. They ignored impossibilities. A man, dying alone, has a vision. He dies. But the entire vision is recorded by a writer who was not present. In class, I kept making comparisons with Tacitus.

Suddenly someone realized the problem. They were believers. They had been taught to accept the Bible, not to examine it; to believe, not to question.

Thus we reached the third bias: the bias of the reader. Once it was clearly stated, they could proceed. And we made it clear that believing in miracles was a matter of faith and thus beyond the scope of the historian to test for verity.

*　　　　*　　　　*

Fenton and his colleagues had developed a set of lessons that clearly helped students to learn these basic skills. The assignments went on with different readings on the appearance of a great cross in the sky to convert the Emperor Constantine. Then students would read six different interpretations of the decline of the Roman Empire. But whatever they read, it was not just for the factual account; the purpose was to learn skills.

It works. Not with every student, but with many. They learn to read with care, to make notes with precision, to approach an author looking for his or her credentials and sources and mechanics of argument.

It is an excellent beginning to a history class. That beginning needs review and reuse and resharpening. Practice. Practice. In time, the students can even apply the methods to the advertising for automobiles and the huckstering of political candidates. They are learning to be critical thinkers.

And for the teacher, it is fun. Each class becomes a new delight, more so because the students are taking a delight in it. For me, this was a big step toward learning how to teach.

Moreover, students learned to write. A favorite essay question given in advance went something like this: What biases have you learned to watch out for in the study of history? Give examples other than those used in class.

Each paper turned in must have the student's name on the back, only on the back. This broke a long tradition, for most of them had always written their names on the front of the paper for twelve years of public school. But I would not tell them why. I made them tell me why, and they quickly caught on. "The bias of the reader," one student shouted out. I wanted to grade their papers only on what they had written, not what I knew they usually did or how well they spoke up in class or how good-looking or pleasant they were. What counts is what is written.

Please don't get the notion that these classes did not learn "the facts of history," the events in sequence and with some sense of causation and linkage. They were assigned plenty of short essays, brief paragraphs on key topics on which they were to report as a news reporter might: who? what? when? where? why? And they were pressed to get events in order without just memorizing dates. Their writing improved.

I don't want to mislead any teacher here. Assigning essay tests means many hours of reading and grading. It also means that the teacher has to organize the appropriate answer in advance, in outline form, and use that as a yardstick for grading. It takes hours.

Often students complained: "We do more writing for your class than for English classes." "Well, aren't you the lucky ones!" And when they actually compared the type of writing done for each class, they discovered that the history classes provided them with thousands of facts from which to select and organize and write. English classes quite often asked the students to generate their own data and then select and organize and write.

Teaching history is really teaching about language. So is teaching almost any subject.

*   *   *

Seeking the bias of the writer or the bias of his or her sources or recognizing your own bias becomes a never-ending employment. We do get better at the first two with practice. But the third will always give us problems.

Moreover, the teacher can introduce the hunt for bias at any time; the teacher can teach that critical skill many, many times during a quarter. It is needed.

Remember: Don't tell them, let them discover. What we discover for ourselves lasts a long time; what we are told vanishes into our notes. One carries meaning; the other does not.

And you lecturers, you can take a few slight risks, just a few minimal ventures into the world of student intellectuality. I promise you, you will be astonished at how bright some of your students are. And those who shine may not always be those with the best recall.

5

Coping with Rigid Beliefs: Ribs and Amulets

"He has a binary view of the world," said Mrs. Craig of her husband, the arrogant doctor in "St. Elsewhere." "There are two possible views on any subject: his view and the wrong one."

A teacher must be aware that a class of forty students will surely include several young Craigs whose early training in stringent doctrine has led to beliefs that brook no deviation and encourage no tolerance.

How do you teach students about a topic that they have been told a hundred times is the work of the Devil?

You sneak up on them.

When I first taught physical anthropology in a small junior college in Rochester, I quickly found that giving a lecture titled "Evidences for Evolution" was inviting turmoil.

So instead, I had the class meet in the zoology lab, seating five or six at a table. Each table displayed one mounted skeleton: a fish, a frog, a baby crocodile, a chicken, a cat, a monkey, or a human being. The students were to make simple sketches of each skeleton, not artistic drawings, just straight lines for straight bones, curved lines for curved bones.

"Be sure to count the bones while you sketch them. In five minutes you will shift tables. And label your drawings so that you

58

can tell the monkey from the frog. Some of you don't draw any better than I do."

By the third shift, one could detect a different tone in the class noise. Yelps of astonishment announced that someone had discovered that the frog had five fingers and so did the monkey. Or that both the cat and the human had one bone in the upper arm, two in the lower, a cluster of bones in the wrist plus five digits. Sometimes the fifth toe was a nubbin or a dewclaw.

Students would rush back to see a skeleton again. They were discovering comparative anatomy and sharing all the delights of discovery. They saw the similarity in spinal columns, in ribs, in shoulder blades, in hips, in skulls, in teeth. They saw; they counted; they learned; they drew; they generalized. The noise level rose as they helped each other to learn.

I nagged at them to draw sketches.

Of the five types of evidence for evolution, they learned a bit of comparative anatomy and were exposed to a bit about vestigial remains. Later would come lessons on blood types, fossils, and comparative embryology.

This first lesson they remembered well because they had discovered it themselves.

*   *   *

"Is that the skeleton of a man or a woman?" Same lesson, several years later. I reined in my impulse to show off my knowledge.

"This class ought to be able to tell. You should know what to look for. Come on, who can help? How can we tell whether this is a skeleton of a man or a woman?"

"The pelvis is wider in women."

"The shoulders are wider in men."

"Men are taller."

Then the arguments rose over whether such general statements could apply to one individual. One big woman chuckled throughout.

A voice came from the rear. "Just count the ribs."

Several laughed. I blinked, then waved him forward. "Come on up, count them."

He counted twelve ribs on each side, then asked me, "How many are there supposed to be?"

At that point, the argument really began. Men had one rib fewer on their left side. No, men had fewer ribs on both sides. No, men had the same number of ribs as women. When student nurses tried to explain what they had learned in anatomy class, they were ignored or shouted down.

The problem for the teacher is not necessarily to know some truth, helpful though that can be, but to figure out how students can learn.

"This is not a question of opinion. It is not a question of belief. It is a question of fact. Men and women exist. They have ribs. You can count them. Count your own."

Counting your own ribs leads to confusion.

Counting someone else's ribs leads to giggling.

We needed another method.

The real question was, how could they determine for themselves? How could they remove any doubt without yielding to an authority, such as a nurse, a doctor, or a textbook? How could they count?

At long last, someone thought of x-rays.

Next day, a nurse brought in two large brown envelopes of chest x-rays, six of men, six of women. She taped the women's to the windowpane; I taped the men's.

The class counted. Everyone counted. We tallied our counts publicly on the blackboard.

They kept counting twelve ribs on the right side of the men and twelve on the left side of the men.

They kept counting twelve ribs on the right side of the women and twelve on the left side of the women.

Finally, all argument ceased. They accepted the answer.

*   *   *

As for the mounted skeleton that prompted the hubbub, we found a smooth forehead with no bony supraorbital ridges above the eyes, a smooth occiput with no bony bumps on the back of the head, and a pretty large pelvis. We settled on a female—"probably."

Getting some people to admit "probably" is a big step.

Then I tried to get the class to state in words what they had done. They had agreed on what to count. They had counted in front of each other. A simple bit of operationalism had resolved an argument.

*   *   *

Weeks later, I returned to the rib question. Most of the students seemed to understand simple operationalism. Define what you mean, agree on a definition, and then count.

"And what types of questions could you not settle by using an operational method, by defining, by looking, and by counting?"

Soon they settled on questions of taste and questions of belief. One student explained: "If you argue over whether ghosts are tall, scaly, and purple instead of small, fuzzy, and misty, you will never settle the argument, because nobody has ever seen a ghost."

"Hey, they have, too. Lots of people have seen ghosts."

Later the two agreed that they could not agree on what to count, a big step for the believer in ghosts. They had less trouble on questions of a preference for rare steak, ski trips, jazz music, or the color blue.

*   *   *

I later recounted the rib incident to a thoracic surgeon, Jim Clagett of the Mayo Clinic. He grinned at me. "You might have had a more exciting class discussion if one of those x-rays had turned up with thirteen pairs of ribs. It does happen. Or only eleven."

"On men or women?"

"Either."

"Where is the extra rib?"

"Usually on the seventh cervical. It grows out above the collarbones and interferes with muscles and blood vessels. I've taken out lots of them."

*   *   *

Early in the quarter, the students all wrote a brief paragraph in answer to a problem. Later we discussed their answers. Here's the problem: "The world has just been invaded from outer space. All major capitals of the world have been shielded from the sun by a black cloud. The United Nations has been given an ultimatum."

The class smirks; I try not to.

"This is the ultimatum. The invaders are carnivorous; they want meat to eat. They are willing to let us survive if we concentrate on raising animals for them to eat. The problem is that they cruise about in small airships, drop nets with hooks on any animal that looks tasty, and then reel up fresh dinner. They don't want to eat us by mistake. Neither do we want that.

"Therefore, they need a description of human beings that will protect us from mistakes. Each of you write a description of a human being that clearly separates us from the other animals."

Here are some answers. The comments were made later at the end of the quarter when we discussed the answers.

1. Man is a two-legged animal with no hair except on top of his head. He wears clothes and uses tools.

Comments: A hairy-armed man objected. A balding man objected. A mother of a baby objected. A sunbather objected.

2. Man is the only rational animal.

Comments: Maybe sometimes, but how could the aliens tell?

3. Man is the only animal with a soul.

Comments: How could you prove that in a hurry?

4. Man is the animal that cooks his food, speaks a language, wears clothing, and uses tools.

Comments: That might save some people some of the time.

5. Just ask the question: "Are you a human being?" If the answer is yes, don't eat them. It's really very simple.

Comments: Is the question in French, Russian, Swahili, Spanish, or any of 3,000 other languages? How about babies? Deaf people? Helen Keller?

What's the point to such discussions? It means using your knowledge. It means thinking critically. And since no names were read aloud, it means revising your own ideas without embarrassment.

At this late period in the quarter, some of the students realized that we were composing an operational definition of humankind. No class ever succeeded. But the process was fun.

*   *   *

On the first day of a class in anthropology, I usually gave a quiz. "Mark each statement true or false to the best of your knowledge or belief." Here are some of the statements:

1. A blood transfusion from a Negro to a Norwegian would turn the Norwegian's skin dark. And the Norwegian might have children with dark skin.

2. Prehistoric man lived about the time of the dinosaurs.

3. The world was created about 4004 B.C.

4. On the ceiling of the Sistine Chapel, Michelangelo painted Adam without a navel.

5. A white woman who marries a man who looks white but actually has one-sixty-fourth Negro ancestry could have a very black child, a throwback.

6. The major civilizations of the world have all begun in temperate climates.

7. An ape is more like a human being than it is like a monkey.

8. On intelligence tests in World War I, whites on the average scored higher than Negroes on the average.

9. On intelligence tests in World War I, northern Negroes on the average scored higher than southern whites.

10. Intelligence tests measure how smart you are: They measure your ability, not your education.

If you guess that some of these were designed to be provocative, you're right.

When we retested and discussed at the end of the quarter, the class had been exposed to nearly all of the relevant facts needed to deal with those questions.

Some students used their knowledge this second time. Some did not. A few in every class regarded "book learning" as an utter

ırrelevancy. They lived in two worlds: their real world of the prejudices reinforced by their friends, and then the "nutty junk" they
had to learn to get by in a class. One of the functions of education
is to force a student to confront the two, to make him or her aware
of the contradictions between verifiable knowledge and everyday
attitudes. Or to help that student climb another rung on the ladder
that William Perry and his friends built.

The most effective persuader is another student, a peer. I kept
quiet. I refereed, trying never to say "That's right" or "That's
wrong."

Remember when the blood banks segregated blood? The fear
of blood from another race was strong in the thirties and forties.
The notion died a quick death in one class after a Korean War
veteran spoke up.

He was blond, blue-eyed, rugged, and very composed. When
a fearful student was spouting off about the dangers of blood trans-
fusions, the vet cut him off. "I never heard such nonsense from a
man who can read and write. Let me tell you. When I was wounded,
I passed out from loss of blood. I woke up in a MASH unit lying
on my back with needles and tubes in me. On the cot next to me
was a big, husky black soldier giving me his blood. The nicest sight
I've ever seen. A beautiful sight. And since I came home, we've had
three daughters. All blonds. Don't spread any more of your ignorant
racism around here."

The other guy was just smart enough to shut up.

Later, a student pointed out that the "Norwegian" might
possibly be black, since nationality does not define race. I revised
the test to read "blond Norwegian."

An old dog can learn.

After discussion, most of the students ended up supporting
questions 7, 8, and 9 as true and all the rest as false. The fun came
with the arguments, not with the conclusions. The learning came
with the arguments.

*   *   *

Of all the values that my students carried into the classroom,
the most thoroughly entrenched were those linked to the Bible and
to what they had learned in a church.

Alec followed me into my office right after class, disturbed, but unable to tell me why. Finally he blurted out that this class contradicted the Bible. I asked him in what way it did. He didn't know, but it did.

"We have Bibles in the library. Go check some out, bring them here, and show me."

He refused. Someone might see him carrying a Bible. So I crossed the hall, checked out a King James, a Douay, and a Goodspeed and told him which was which. He sat down to read Genesis. And he did know that Genesis was in the front of the book.

He began. Quickly he found that the three were different in language. He flipped back to the title pages with a worried look. Then he stared at me with great indignation.

"You said this was a Catholic Bible and it isn't." He held the Douay in his hand.

"Yes, it is, it was translated into English in the French town of Douay, and copies were smuggled into England when Queen Elizabeth was . . ."

"No. This is not the Catholic Bible. I can tell. I know."

"How can you tell?"

"Because this one has the New Testament. The New Testament is about Jesus, and Catholics don't believe in Jesus."

He was triumphant. I was in shock.

"I know lots about Catholics. I teach about other religions, been teaching for three years now. I know lots about them."

"Teaching? Where?"

"In Sunday school. I teach the fifth grade." He named a large Protestant church.

Ten minutes later, I had partially convinced him that he was confusing Catholics with Jews. That made no difference to Alec; he disliked both, though he was not sure why. His ignorance of Martin Luther, Erasmus, the papacy, Henry VIII, John Calvin, the Diaspora, the Holocaust, and the Reformation was total.

One moral of this story is that when you recruit volunteers, you had better screen them for their personal motives and abilities.

Slowly, Alec and I got back to Genesis and his problem with my class. I asked him to read carefully and to get the order of creation in chapter one. He did that. Then he began with the order of creation in chapter two, starting with verse four, where the second story begins. Alec was to write them down on paper.

Alec was my first such case but by no means my last encounter with those whose ignorance is matched only by their cocksureness and their ethnocentrism. Most students who talked about this in my office could accept the Bible as great literature and history and inspiration and poetry and metaphor. Some like Alec, the literalists, wanted to pound others into agreement or submission. They wanted to clobber the unbeliever with the Bible until he or she would agree or be quiet. Some were fundamentalists, some were Jesus freaks, some were "born again." Many of them seemed to be Pharisees.

Here is what Alec wrote:

Day 1. light, day, night
Day 2. the firmament (Heaven) out of the waters
Day 3. the land out of the seas, grass, herbs, trees
Day 4. sun, moon, stars
Day 5. fowl, whales, living creatures
Day 6. cattle, creeping things, beasts, man and woman
Day 7. rest

And here is what Alec did for the second list.

Day 1. earth and heavens
every plant
every herb
mist
man out of dust
garden, tree of life, tree of knowledge
gold, bdellium, onyx
four rivers
beasts to be named by Adam
Eve from Adam's rib

Poor Alec was puzzled. When he read the two other translations and found them much the same, he was more puzzled than ever. It was too much for him. Genesis had become a problem when he wanted a revelation.

"How do you explain this?"

"Alec, that is not my business. I'm not going to explain the Bible to you. All I insist on is that if you quote it to me in a discussion, you quote it accurately. Someplace in there is a rule that you should not bear false witness."

That did not cheer him up.

"Now we still have the problem you came in here with: the disagreement between your text and your lists here. Do you want to discuss that? Or do you want to read some more?"

He just looked unhappy.

"Or you might read chapter five of Genesis for a third story of creation."

"Huh?"

"Well, it's up to you. And you might look up the difference between the *J* and the *E* versions. Try some good encyclopedia or perhaps the introduction to one of the modern translations. I faintly recall that the *J* stands for Jehovah and the *E* for Elohim, but I'm not sure. You look it up and tell me. But tell me in my office. I'm not qualified to teach religion in a class, and I certainly do not want to impose religious views on a class. Not your views and not mine."

Several days later, Alec actually reported back to me on the *J* and *E* versions and how they had been combined. The different translations bothered him. Since he had never learned any other language, he assumed that words could be directly translated from one language into another. He knew nothing about idioms or metaphors or historical shifts in the usage of words.

We settled on one point. He was to study the assigned text and to answer the questions according to the course material. His duty was to understand, not to believe.

Each quarter, I had several Alecs. Most spoke up only in my office; a few challenged me in class. Usually a referral to talk with their minister was sufficient, but not always.

*　　　*　　　*

When my boss retired, he called me in and showed me a file folder. "I just wanted you to see the heat that I've been taking for you these seven years. These are letters of complaint or memos of phone calls about you."

I read through the file. They came from ministers, priests, parents, and students. They said, variously, that I was incompetent, unqualified, an atheist, a Communist, a Republican, a Democrat, a Lutheran, a Catholic, a Jew, and a few other things, some of them even nasty.

"Why didn't you tell me?"

"You were busy teaching. Taking complaints is my job. Of course, if I had thought that you were really off limits, I might have said something. Just think what this college would be like if we taught only what all parents could agree on—the lowest common denominator."

In later years, with a new administration, every complaint was routinely transferred to me. That was okay, too. I like to know what the critics say. They did not change much.

Where would you place Alec on the nine-point Perry scale? Where would you place my boss who took the complaints?

*   *   *

The Bible surfaced as a problem for many students through the years. Some students asked concerned questions, and I found that my best answer was that I was not teaching religion; they should talk with their minister. Most of the ministers dealt easily with literature, poetry, metaphor, and various translations without being swamped in literalism.

When Catholic students still had a problem, I might suggest that they read Père Teilhard de Chardin. Teilhard was the French priest-archaeologist who helped in the famous dig near Peking, China, and also found a bone at the Piltdown site and thus unwittingly lent his name and prestige to a famous hoax.

Teilhard wrote in such murky prose that no one could really disagree with him.

Many of my students who had gone to their church leaders with such concerns came back with an explanation that the Bible contained an enormously diverse body of stories and history and poetry and census records and prophecies and that they were not to worry. Those who were told to worry seldom reported to me.

After the encounter with Alec, I learned to keep a Bible in my office, ready at my hand for those purveyors of final truths. The copy I kept was my own, with my name in gold on the cover, a gift at confirmation from Lester Park Methodist Church in Duluth.

In affirming your credibility, the little touches count.

*   *   *

Betty edged hesitantly through the door to my office. Something was troubling her. With a bit of encouragement, she blurted out that she could not take the tests because she knew that everything she wrote was false. Betty could not accept "this stuff about fossils." Tests made her so tense that she was failing them. Sunday school was interfering again.

On my bookcase was a grubby little candy box filled with fossil seashells. I had picked them up at a local quarry northeast of town from the Platteville limestone stratum, about twenty-one feet thick. One pretty little bivalve lay on top. I placed it on the table. "Take a look."

She stared, not daring to touch. Touching that mineralized seashell would contaminate her in some unknown way. The fears learned in childhood are deep.

I set the shell on a Kleenex tissue and gave her a small magnifying glass. "Take a close look. It's just a tiny little seashell from Quarry Hill. It came from the years when Minnesota was under the ocean."

She looked. She poked it with a pencil. She picked it up in the tissue. She magnified it with the glass. She was conquering her fear, gradually.

"Are you ready for the test tomorrow?"

"I've studied. But I get so tensed up that I can't write."

"Here is something to help." I wrapped the fossil seashell in the tissue. "You need not touch it. Just carry it in your purse and bring it to the exam."

"Just carry it in my purse?"

"When you begin to tense, take three deep breaths and relax

after each one. Hold this in your left hand. You can leave it wrapped up."

"What will that do?" She giggled.

"Do you believe in magic?"

"No." And she giggled again.

"Neither do I, but sometimes this works. Just hold it. Take deep breaths. Relax. You'll be okay. Remember, take three deep breaths, then relax."

During the test next day, she held the fossil, wrapped, in her hand. She smiled a small, uncertain smile. And she passed the test.

Two weeks later, she let me see her unwrapping the fossil to hold in her bare hand. This time she flashed a big smile.

Six months later, on graduation night, Betty told me that she still kept the fossil in her purse. It was now her amulet. It helped her in every test, holding anxiety at bay, reminding her to relax.

Away from the punch bowl, I gave her a quickie talk on Joseph Wolpe and his desensitization methods for overcoming fears through a graded series of behaviors whereby you come closer and closer to the thing you fear. When the tension mounts, you practice relaxation and deep breathing. Using these methods, therapists can overcome fears of snakes, heights, airplanes, swimming, sex, nudity, public speaking, or eating sushi.

Or fear of very dead seashells. Or fear of ideas.

*   *   *

Linking human beings to other animals is not just for purposes of taxonomy, of classification, although that is certainly a valuable scientific exercise.

There is a grander concept. Understanding that we share blood types with the apes and monkeys, that we share reproductive design with other mammals, that we share skeletal design with other vertebrates, that we are part of the same food chain, and that our teeth indicate that our long-ago ancestors were vegetarians more often than they were carnivores shows our kinship. We breathe the same air as the other animals; we drink the same water as they do; and we are poisoned by the same pollution. Our destiny is linked with other life. We are human beings, we are primates, we are mammals, we are vertebrates, we are part of the grand scheme of life on earth.

We are kin to other life forms and are bound to them by genetic links that we are barely beginning to comprehend. We are a part of life on our planet. We belong here.

How does one teach such a concept to freshmen?

Loren Eisely conveyed this notion beautifully, writing in prose almost like poetry. Jacques Cousteau, in many films, has communicated a similar vision of our place in nature.

For most students, the insight came incrementally as they saw, bit by bit, the statuses that we have held in nature. From gatherer and scavenger to hunter, we have slowly changed to planter of wheat and barley, planter of maize and squash and beans, planter of rice and soybeans. We became tamer of animals and then breeders of domesticated dogs and sheep and pigs and cattle and horses. We have become diggers of the earth and makers of roads and builders of canals and of vast terraced gardens for rice and for corn.

But we have dumped waste into our gardens and poisoned our wells. We have fouled the air with smog. Now we threaten all life with nuclear war or the slower threat of nuclear waste.

When we threaten each other, we threaten all life on earth, for we are kin to all life, even sharing the molecular design of DNA with lettuce and oak trees and butterflies.

A class would handle plaster casts of the fossil skulls of early humans. Often we could simply array them in order of size, from the small skull of the *Australopithecus* to the larger skull of the *Homo erectus* of Peking or the even larger one from Java. Bigger yet was the Neanderthal's skull, and then the skull of the modern human, with a slightly smaller cranial capacity.

Our smaller brain size always leads to a discussion of whether we are actually smarter than the Neanderthals were. No one really knows, of course. But we did survive, and they did not. However, the Neanderthals were a very successful species who spread their physical type and their culture over Europe, Russia, Asia, and Africa; they invented a full kit of excellent stone tools; they practiced unknown rituals in dim caves, setting bear skulls in magic circles or boxing them in stone crypts; they buried their own dead in elaborate rituals, bidding them farewell with gifts of food and weapons and decorating graves with ibex horns or wild flowers. And they endured for 100,000 years, which is more than we have done or yet may do.

Since I first began reading about early humans in the 1920s and then took my first class under Fay Cooper Cole in 1935, the paleontologists have upgraded the Neanderthals. Back then, they were described as low-browed and brutish, unable to stand fully erect, shambling about in damp caves. They were the cavemen of the cartoons.

More careful study has shown that they did not walk in a crouch. They and our own types possibly interbred. At least, caves in Palestine contain fossils of each type and also of some intermediate forms. Their bigger brains make them far more acceptable, despite our snobbery.

Our shift in attitude is revealed in the way scientists label the two types now. Once we called ourselves *Homo sapiens,* "the wise man," a label reserved only for us. But now we have included the Neanderthals; they are *Homo sapiens neanderthalensis.* To maintain a whiff of distinction, we added another *sapiens* to our name. We are now officially *Homo sapiens sapiens,* "the wise, wise man."

Ah, humility.

Including the Neanderthals as *Homo sapiens* gives our species another 100,000 years of prehistory. And it widens the definition of being human. Of course, those who cannot feel kinship for a person of another race will hardly feel kinship with Neanderthals.

Bit by bit, the students would see these linkages of humankind to other animals.

The first mammal we sent into space was a chimpanzee named Ham. The description of his early flight and the reasons given for sending a chimpanzee echoed the class in physical anthropology. Skeleton, blood types, muscles, nerves, brain, digestion, all these were similar in both species. Ham was like us. Ham was very like us.

Since the advent of television, much of this material on primates and on fossil finds has become popular. Millions of people know about Jane Goodall and her wild chimpanzees or about Don

Johanson and Lucy or about Louis and Mary Leakey and Richard Leakey and their many fossil finds in Africa.

Increasing public knowledge stirred a reaction from the fundamentalists and the literalists. They poured money into publicizing "creationism" as a science and labeling scientific attitudes as "secular humanism," which they then attacked. They persuaded several state legislatures to require teaching "creationism" in science classes.

When such issues arose in my class, I found that the old methods worked: State your evidence clearly, give your sources, discuss openly which theory best explains the facts.

We need more than Dr. Craig's binary view of the world. We need far more than the arrogant assertion of absolute truth. In a world of flux, we must prepare young people to solve problems for which there is no answer in the back of the book.

Plenty of others are scrambling to teach students what to think.

Our job is to teach them how to think.

6

Testing Hypotheses: Bare Feet

College students once had a fad of wearing shoes but no socks. Winter and summer, bare ankles winked at me from beneath ragged blue denim. In my 8 A.M. sociology class, I asked why. A sockless student answered that socks were uncomfortable, that bare feet were cooler.

"But this is January."

He shrugged. "It's more comfortable."

Others disagreed. Those without socks became loudly defensive when accused of yielding to peer pressure. Not by coincidence, peer pressure was discussed in the chapter assigned for the day. The socked and the sockless each thought the other was yielding to peer pressure.

I shifted the focus. "How could we test whether it is more comfortable or not? How could socks be proved to be more or less comfortable than no socks?"

"We could ask a lot of people; we could take a survey."

"Naw, it's too personal. We'd just be collecting opinions."

"We could wear socks one day and not the next."

Since I had a method in mind, I kept prodding, bringing up the analogy of studies in which identical twins are separated and then checked for differences due to environment.

Someone caught the hint.

74

"Hey, our feet are just like twins. We could wear one sock only and leave the other foot bare."

In a few minutes, the students set up the experiment. The whole class would walk about the next day with a sock on only one foot. Each would wear two shoes. Every hour on the hour, each person would record which foot felt most comfortable. We all wrote down a chart for the record.

When the most vociferous sockless student objected that all the reports except his would be biased, another sockless one pointed out that this was a superb opportunity to convert the entire class.

Wednesday the class met again. Each wore only one sock— all but three of us. The original vociferous sockless one refused to participate in anything as stupid as that experiment. Another sockless one had forgotten. I had worn two deliberately until class time. I took one off and lent it to the forgetful one.

He wore my sock all day as we all took notes. He showed up at my office in the afternoon, grinning, and returned my sock.

The next day, the sock borrower wore socks on both feet. But my goal was not to persuade him to conform. I was frying other fish.

I shall not here relate the remarks from my colleagues that day, nor those of students from other classes when they saw my one bare ankle. Sometimes we scientists must suffer scorn as we search for the great universal truths hidden in the cosmos.

On Friday, we tallied the responses. We did it slowly, calling out the hour, counting the votes, and writing the tally on the blackboard. The tallies mounted slowly and lopsidedly.

Which Foot Felt More Comfortable?

Time	Socked Foot	Sockless Foot
8 A.M.	27	0
9 A.M.	24	0
10 A.M.	27	0
11 A.M.	19	0
12 P.M.	26	0
1 P.M.	25	0
	148	0

The subtotals were uneven because a few had forgotten to record each hour.

The student who refused to participate thought that the whole thing was an elaborate device to pressure him into conforming, a ganging up of peer pressure. It certainly had that effect. I praised him for his independence. However, my real goal was the notion of testing a hypothesis.

*   *   *

Now let me explain the logic of that simple little experiment, whose logic is perfectly clear to you already. But that's the way teachers operate, so let me explain in different terms. Be patient.

Samuel Stouffer, one of my teachers at the University of Chicago, did not invent the four-celled analysis, but he did manage to make it clear to me. Here is the way it goes.

A social scientist wishes to find out whether some factor or influence really does affect people. Do movies change attitudes? Does advertising work? Does stress cause problems in workers? Does alcohol affect one's ability to drive a car? Are feet more comfortable with socks or without?

You get two similar groups of people to study and to measure. You might take a group and arbitrarily divide it into two; you might select two at random; you might carefully match two groups in many variables. Anyway, somehow or other you come up with two groups that are similar to each other. You designate one as the experimental group and the other as the control group. And then you measure both to make sure that they are actually similar on the key factor that you are concerned with.

Then you do something to the experimental group, what you do depending on what theory you are trying to test. You show them a snuff movie or you have them take their exam in an overheated, underventilated room or you have them listen to a partisan political speech or you ply them with liquor. You expose them to some factor that may change their attitude or their ability in a way that you can measure. You might even remove one sock.

Then you measure both groups again.

Now you have four sets of scores—experimental group and

control group before the experiment and after. The four sets make up the four cells of the diagram.

Group	Number Comfortable Before	Number Comfortable After
Experimental	27	0
Control	27	27

So we had two sets of feet, quite well matched. We introduced one variable, removing the sock, and we collected the data by judging the comfort (granted that the measuring device we used was an opinion, or a subjective judgment).

Okay, so you could have told me this without going through this kind of mumbo jumbo. Fine. But. But.

Most research is not quite as simple as this little absurdity.

Most research ends up with small shades of difference, because it is so doggone hard to weed out the variables and the leakages and the contaminants. One researcher told me that when his graduate students tried to assess the influence of one rather simple factor, they most often produced no significant differences. Research can be very frustrating. Also, there are lots of wrong ways to do it.

What good is it?

It's the only way to prove to someone else that your theory works.

Also, this slow accumulation of specific facts is one effective way to convince people. It is about the only way to make them change a prejudice. But don't count on that. Few of us change our prejudices rationally.

After our sockless episode, several students observed that they had tried to argue students not in our class into wearing socks because of the experiment. They had failed. One must go through the stages of setting a problem and collecting data. A conclusion given to you is not yours; it does not convince. This great truth we all learn many times.

*   *   *

Another example, a quickie: One class resented my using pop quizzes once or twice a week. One student led this protest by claiming that the quizzes were an insult to their maturity. Obviously, I didn't trust them to study regularly.

I agreed that I did not trust them to study regularly. "It is a basic principle of learning. If you learn something well enough to be tested on it the first day and then review it for the test three weeks later and then review again for the final exam, you will remember it longer."

They did not want to learn anything that well.

"Your grades will be higher."

"We are adults, capable of making our own decisions."

We set up an experiment. Since I had two sections of the same class, I would drop the quiz for one and keep it for the other. Then we would compare results on the tests. The section still taking the quizzes we labeled the "student section"; the protesting section was the "mature adult section."

On the first such test, the two sections had had similar scores. Since we always worked out the mean, the median, and the mode for practice after every quiz and test, we already had those three measures of central tendency for the first test that quarter:

	Mature Adult Section	Student Section
Mean	82	80
Median	81	80
Mode	74	86

The mode is the least reliable of the three when dealing with small frequencies. Four students earned scores of 74; three students earned 86.

In the next three weeks, to my jaundiced eye, the quality of class discussion dropped considerably in the mature adult section. References to material covered in the text were met with blank faces and hasty turning of pages. Whenever I referred to the students as adults, they grinned self-consciously.

Testing time. Both sections took the same test. However, since the student section had learned about the experiment from the "adults," there did arise a certain competitive spirit, which I hoped would limit the leakage of answers in the hour between classes.

Both sections clamored for the results. Here they are:

	Mature Adult Section	*Student Section*
Mean	68	82
Median	67	83
Mode	88	92

Suddenly the adult section became subdued; in fact, they wanted quizzes. To my jaundiced eye, they had matured.

Now that piece of data gathering is not earning kudos in the research journals. Crude as it was, it confirmed our old knowledge that frequent learning and frequent review means that we remember longer. The psychologist Hermann Ebbinghaus showed that in some classical experiments on memory and forgetting over sixty years ago.

However, neither of the sections seized eagerly on my suggestion of a two-day comprehensive exam covering all of their college studies after the first two years plus a three-day exam covering all of their studies after four years of college. The student nurses, after all, took state boards covering all of their classes. Law students took state bar exams. Medical students took state boards. Many of the professions required a comprehensive exam, and some required an update. If it works for the professions, why not for the rest of us?

* * *

Data gathering by students also has the effect of convincing them. The effect is slow, cumulative, and very persuasive.

When Joe McCarthy of Wisconsin was accusing many citizens of being Communists or homosexuals or both, I turned one class loose on collecting the data on Joe's accusations. They were each to start with one name, one person, and trace the case back in the papers to see what had happened after Joe had attacked that person. They could use newspapers, news magazines, articles, but they must write down their sources with dates so that others could check on them. Each filled out three-by-five cards:

Name of person
Date of accusation
Nature of accusation
Response of the accused
Result: conviction, jail term, dismissal, or charges dropped

The class began their witch-hunt with zeal. This was fun; they were helping to defend the nation. Soon they had a dozen cards with names and accusations. They ended with twenty-two cards, each with a different name of someone accused by Joe. However, the names dropped from the news. They could not determine the outcome of the case.

I told them to keep digging in the library, to keep reading the newspapers.

Bit by bit, they built up a file of completed cards. Bit by bit, the angry denials and then the neglect showed up. McCarthy's accusation made headlines. The victim's denial made a smaller story on page 2. Then McCarthy moved on to a new victim, leaving the first one squirming and denying, searching for a reporter who would listen. Occasionally, a summary story or an analytical article would reveal that the victims were still working, still struggling with the smear, still fighting to find a forum from which to fight back.

The students filled out more cards. And as they worked, a subtle change came over them; they were not finding any Communists. McCarthy had not found any Communists. In all of his long list of victims, none had been proved to be anything but politically more liberal than Joe.

Each day in class, we spent a few minutes discussing their research. After a month, no one had yet found a single name of a real suspect.

One student got angry. Charlie contributed little to the class, but he seemed to know in his heart that McCarthy was right in his crusade. He wrote to the senator asking for help. Senator Joe McCarthy's office responded with a thick package of reprints of speeches and news clippings. Proudly, Charlie came into class with his two manila envelopes stuffed with material. Every day, he carried them to class until someone spoke aloud that fatal conclusion that Joe McCarthy was a fraud.

Charlie rose up in wrath. Here it was, the real story. He pulled out material and began pawing through it.

"I've got plenty of names. Names of real Communists. Here's one: George C. Marshall."

The class hooted. General Marshall, the top general in World War II, then secretary of state, had been discussed many times in class. They pulled out their notes. They read them aloud. They utterly rejected Charlie.

But Charlie would not quit. By then, he had another name. When that was rejected, he pulled another. We could see by his scrambling through many unread booklets that Charlie had never read his material before, and he was not listening to any of the denials.

"You're acting just like McCarthy," one student suggested.

Charlie grew livid. "McCarthy is right!" he yelled. "Only the reds are against him. I'm going to tell him about this class. After all, he was the one that put Alger Hiss in jail." Charlie was the only person in the room who did not know that Alger Hiss had been accused by Whittaker Chambers long before McCarthy began his crusade. Richard Nixon, who then was on the House Committee on Un-American Activities, had led that move.

The slow accumulation of facts works a change in attitude only on those who work through the slow accumulation of facts. Changing our mental patterns is slow, painful, and personal; we can seldom do it vicariously.

*   *   *

When I told colleagues about the experiment on frequent quizzes, one snorted in disgust.

"Frequent review is a waste of time. They can learn it the first time."

His final exam did not cover the whole course, just the last five chapters of the text.

One administrator wanted to reduce the four days for final exams to two days, with only one hour per exam.

"When I was teaching, I always found that the most valuable way to spend exam time was in a class discussion over what was significant in the class."

Much later, we learned that he had taught for one year.

Another colleague laughed about the socks and sockless experiment.

"You goofed that one up, you know. You should have controlled the type of sock that people wore. I can't wear wool socks, only nylon."

"But they chose their own sock, one that they were comfortable with."

"No difference. You lost your control."

7

Discovering Assumptions: Human Nature

"You can't change human nature."

"You can't teach an old dog new tricks."

"What did you expect, human nature being what it is?"

Someone who says that you cannot change human nature must have some idea of the human nature that cannot be changed. It is the key to the puzzle of most great literature, all of the social sciences, and the humanities. You English teachers know what I mean. What is the nature of human nature?

Here is one answer, from Machiavelli (1952, p. 98), the Italian who wrote *The Prince,* a handbook on how to be a strong one way back in 1513. "For of men it may generally be affirmed that they are thankless, fickle, false, studious to avoid danger, greedy of gain, devoted to you while you confer benefits upon them and ready, as I said before, while the need is remote to shed their blood, and sacrifice their property, their lives, and their children for you; but when it comes near they turn against you."

So you toss that famous quotation to a class and ask them what they think of it. The cynics will agree. Some of the more idealistic will doubt it. Some will bring up contrary examples of generosity and unselfishness and heroes who died for their country. The cynics will scoff.

83

What is the nature of human nature? And whatever it is, can it be changed?

Did Machiavelli describe you? Your father? Your mother? Your brother?

*   *   *

Consider this next list carefully. The distilled wisdom from the wise ones of the Western world is presented here for your learning. Just think what problems you can solve or avoid if you understand these. They surely shall give you a real insight into the nature of human nature.

1. Give him a taste of his own medicine.
2. Birds of a feather flock together.
3. The end does not justify the means.
4. He who hesitates is lost.
5. A penny saved is a penny earned.
6. Absence makes the heart grow fonder.
7. Opposites attract.
8. Look before you leap.
9. Idleness is the devil's workshop.
10. You can't take it with you.
11. Too many cooks spoil the broth.
12. All work and no play makes Jack a dull boy.
13. A stitch in time saves nine.
14. Haste makes waste.
15. Out of sight, out of mind.
16. Foul means can make fair ends.
17. Two wrongs don't make a right.
18. Many hands make light work.

My classes would stare at such a list and ask what was the point of it. My answer was that I wanted them to take notes on the list, but not till they had determined a good form for taking the notes. That didn't help.

Before you peek at answers, read that list again.

Next, I would ask whether each bit of wisdom was true and

valuable and a help in time of trouble. Then I would get some smarter answers. "It depends." "That varies." When I pressed students about such responses, one of them would point out that if you had a high school sweetheart who went to a different college, then it was problematic whether number 6 or number 15 was valid. Grins around the room, a few rather shamefaced.

Someone else would say that number 11 was true sometimes and number 18 was true at other times and that the best committee was three persons with two of them absent.

That would break the dam. Students would find paired opposites all over and begin calling out the numbers. Thus they determined the form for taking notes: a double column. Each proverb with its paired opposite.

Caution: There are times when teachers who use the inquiry system must break the vows of silence to deliver a moral lecture. This is one.

"Now let me warn you. If your father delights in clinching an argument by quoting one of these, don't pull out your notebook, hunt up the opposing quotation, and slay the poor man. Just smile inwardly. And if your old aunt loves to quote them, don't knock her down, either—particularly if she is rich. Remember what happened to Abelard when he got too smart."

Of course, college freshmen seldom know what happened to Abelard or what Heloise had to do with his later and unhappy circumstances. But with a bit of encouragement, some of them will hunt in the library and return to tell the class. Encourage students to use libraries. That is half the fun.

They never forget the story of Abelard. I tell them that the moral of the story is to be tactful in heckling your teachers. It was Abelard, in *Sic et non* (that is scholarly Latin lingo for "Yes and no"), who made double columns of contradictory arguments in theology and provided students in Paris with an arsenal of arguments for heckling unfortunate professors. Their brutal revenge is part of his unhappy story.

*   *   *

In any discussion in the social sciences, or the humanities, or literature, certain issues arise again and again, usually in a disguised form. The teacher must recognize quickly what assumptions are blocking understanding.

One is ethnocentrism.

Another is racism.

A third is the notion of human instincts, the notion that most significant human behavior is inherited, not learned. It is the old nature-nurture problem. And it is linked to racism because it lays the stress on inherited behavior.

My point here is that many issues are hidden. Students learn assumptions, or absorb them as part of our culture, about all sorts of things: Whites are smarter than blacks or Indians or Hispanics. Men are smarter than women. Americans are patriotic, honest, and brave and would never stoop to deceit, murder, or torture. Nobody ever works unless he or she is paid. America is a Christian country, which is why we are so decent. A woman who is raped must have asked for it. Hang a few murderers and the rest of the crooks will straighten out in a hurry. Children are nasty little beasts who must be domesticated. You can't change human nature. Children are little angels corrupted by a nasty society. What do you expect, human nature being what it is?

Some teachers ignore these questions. Some lecture on these questions. Some present a problem to get students arguing and looking for more information and asking more questions and using the library.

Here is one way. Begin with a simple problem about the nature of instincts. (We will get around to human instincts later on.) Present this on a transparency:

> If you stole an egg from a robin's nest, then hatched the egg in an incubator and fed it and raised it with chicks, would the grown bird sing like a robin, or would it cluck like a chicken?

I've been lucky. Every class has had at least one farm kid who laughs and tells how he has placed pheasant eggs in the chick incubator. They hatch and grow up to look like pheasants and act like pheasants. "But they are sort of tame and not afraid of hunters."

Or a bird watcher who knows about cuckoos and cowbirds

will describe their secretly laying eggs in other birds' nests. The young cuckoo still sounds like a cuckoo, and the cowbird grows up to be a cowbird.

However, canary breeders encourage canaries to sing more by letting them hear good singers. Today they may play tapes to encourage young canaries. The birds do not sing differently, just oftener and with more complexity.

Try the same question on your friends. You may be amazed at their responses. They may be amazed at yours. Everyone has a verdict on the noise from that poor orphaned robin.

How did the chicks in the incubator grow up to cluck like chickens instead of humming like an incubator?

* * *

What is meant by human nature? We talk easily about the nature of dogs, or the nature of cows or bees or monkeys or kittens. Most of us are pretty sure that dogs and cats and cows and monkeys behave pretty much the same way in whatever circumstances life thrusts upon them. We think that they inherit that behavior. Most folks think so. Let's look at some cases. And then let's compare them with human behavior and human nature.

Draw a chalk line across the board. Write "All Instinctive" at one end and "All Learned" at the other. Divide it into intervals to make a crude scale. Now try to agree on where you will put robins on that scale. Where do you put insects? On which side of the robin?

You can describe how the egg of a hunting wasp will hatch underground into a larva that then eats the living meat of a caterpillar that the mother wasp has paralyzed until the larva grows large enough to pupate. Then, after a rest period, it slowly goes through metamorphosis to emerge as an adult wasp that knows exactly how to mate, how to capture a caterpillar, which it paralyzes and into which it lays one egg and which it then buries underground. The egg hatches, the larva eats the living meat that the mother has provided, until it, too, is large enough to pupate and go through metamorphosis to emerge as an adult that knows just what to do. And on and on for generations cycling upon generations. Since I could seldom rely on students knowing many details about insects, I usually just gave a quickie lecture on hunting wasps, basing it on a book by Crompton (1955), *The Hunting Wasp.* Does the wasp learn, or does it inherit all its patterns? Since the new wasp never saw its parent, how could it have been taught? And since the pattern is unchanging, what did it ever learn? And how?

Zip. At the far end of the scale under "All Instinctive." All inherited, nothing learned. Not much argument over that one.

Along in here, I usually supplied a definition of instinctive behavior. This one came from Hunter and Whitten's (1976, p. 217) *Encyclopedia of Anthropology.*

> INSTINCTS. This term broadly used, refers to un-learned behavior occurring in all normal members of a species under identical conditions. In the past, the word *instinct* has been so widely applied to so many different aspects of animal and human behavior—ranging from the simple reflex to the sexual drive—that scientists have been obliged to refine their use of the concept. In general it may be said that the following minimal criteria must be met if a pattern of behavior is to be considered instinctive:
>
> 1. an instinct is genetically encoded, born into the organism and into all members of the same species and cannot be unlearned;
> 2. unlike a simple reflex, an instinct is a complex bundle of behaviors which appears fully developed when first elicited (although an instinct may not be mature at birth);
> 3. an instinct is elicited by specific and unvarying stimuli;
> 4. instincts are goal-directed, typically toward the reduction of internal tension.
>   . . . most social scientists do not find the term useful in the analysis of human behavior.

That is a big mouthful, and it may take a while to understand all those requirements before you can use the word *instinct*

in a scientific sense. So just go on to the next problem, returning
to that big definition whenever needed as we sort out the behavior
of animals with totally instinctive behavior from those who learn
some behavior.

*   *   *

Once more:

A cat will instinctively kill rats. Or must it be taught
to kill?

After hearing some tales of the mother cat bringing in a
wounded mouse to her kittens to kill, you present the setup from
a famous old experiment (Kuo, 1930), but you keep the data
concealed.

	Percentage of Kittens *Becoming Rat Killers*
In first four months kittens witness mother cat killing rats.	—
Kittens do not witness mother cat killing any rats until after four months old.	—
Kittens raised with rats as companions	—

Usually I would ask the students to draw up a hypothesis
before they saw any of the data results. If you accept that killing rats
is instinctive, then what prediction would you make as to the percentages? If you think of the trait as learned behavior, then what
prediction would you make?

Only when predictions have been written down in each notebook, when a class understands the clear connection between results
and theory, do you release the results. The predictions should be
written clearly: "If rat killing by kittens is instinctive, then the
results will be ———." The formula is "If this, then that."

Here are Kuo's results from the top down: 85 percent, 45
percent, and 0 percent for the kittens raised with rats. However,

about 16 percent of that last group did kill other small animals. When a class tries to make sense out of that, they first leap to the "All Learned" end of the scale. Then, with some second thoughts, they accept some inherited patterns, and they also realize that some kittens flunk the course.

Once again, method must be stressed. This is a superb chance to show the relationship of theory to research, of theory to prediction.

Let me nag a little. Most of us teachers are so eager to show off our knowledge that we present all the data and thus muff the chance to let students use their big brains. Remember, guessing the correct percentage of rat killers is quite unimportant compared to understanding theory and understanding how to make predictions on theory and understanding how to test theory.

If this, then that. If you think that this theory is true, then that effect would follow. If we pick an effect that can be measured, we can test our theory. If this, then that.

Just because this chapter is about discovering assumptions, that doesn't mean that we neglect other basic notions of critical thinking. In our run-through on various animal behaviors to fit on our scale, we are beginning to have a mix of inherited patterns and learned patterns and reinforced patterns and repressed patterns. Let the group struggle with it. More will come later to clear up some complexities. And to complicate others.

*   *   *

Harry Harlow, in some famous experiments in his lab at the University of Wisconsin, isolated infant rhesus monkeys by raising each in a box where it could not see out. He found that later they could not cope with other monkeys in playing or in breeding. They were fearful, lonely little animals. In a breeding troop, the alpha male would normally manage to mate with most of the females. But these wretched, isolated females did not know what to do or how and refused to cooperate with an experienced alpha male. The isolated males were equally confused, frightened, and neurotic. Both were afraid of contact with another monkey. They had never been cuddled or carried or nursed or loved; they could not cuddle or carry or nurse or love. Harlow reached one major conclusion: To love, you must have been loved.

When some of these unfortunate females were artificially inseminated, they were utterly incompetent mothers, often rejecting the newborn or killing it. What happened to inherited patterns for reproduction and mothering? Those are important behaviors.

Put rhesus on the scale line between instinct and learning. On which side of the kitten did you put the rhesus?

*   *   *

How do you know where to put the human beings?

Any class in school knows that they are in school to learn skills and attitudes and facts. They also know that the genetic component in their lives has a large effect. Plunge right in with a question: "What instincts do human beings have?" And then you make a list as they call out.

Fighting
Eating
Urinating
Walking
Blushing
Talking
Killing
Self-preservation
Guarding your children
Sexual intercourse

My method usually included writing down stuff that nobody offered but that would provoke discussion. So the list also includes some other items mixed in:

Breathing
Kissing
Hitting with the fist
Sneezing
Loving

Writing
Typing
Filing one's teeth
Stabbing with a spear
Running

Then you go back to the definition of an instinct. Remember that? I would put that on the overhead projector, and the class would examine each item in turn. Does it meet the minimal standards?

Fighting. Apparently most human females are genetically different or maybe deficient. And enough of the males are so deficient that the U.S. Army must draft reluctant young men to fight the wars. The methods of fighting vary. Fists, flat of the hand, edge of the hand, knives, guns, spears, axes, boots, teeth.

Eating. When we are hungry, do we respond by opening the refrigerator, by climbing a tree, or by turning over flat rocks? What determines when we eat, how we eat, or what we eat?

Most of the list items are easy to dispose of. Some are much tougher. Take self-preservation. Your life is at risk. What is your response? Do you run away? Do you swim upward? Do you swerve the car to the shoulder? Do you reach for your rifle? Do you wet a handkerchief to filter the smoke? Do you scream for help? Do you hold your breath?

"That depends."

"Depends on what?"

"That depends on the situation. How is your life being threatened?"

"You mean that your genetic encoding tells you when to reach for a rifle instead of swimming upward?"

Grins of embarrassment. Grins of acceptance. "But I do inherit the desire to keep alive. That's gotta be basic."

"Okay, We all have that. So much so that we usually think that suicide is a sign of sickness or deep depression. The question here is whether it fits our definition of instinct."

*   *   *

"What we need is someone like Harlow to isolate some human babies to determine how they turn out."

Instant protests. "You can't experiment on human beings."

No. You can't. But such things have happened by accident. Children have been abandoned or lost or raised by animals. Most such stories are fiction or so clouded over with myth that you cannot really accept them. Tarzan never lived.

But all my students had been exposed to one famous case, that of Anna. Her story was in every textbook. Anna had been hidden in the attic for seven years because her unwed mother was afraid to reveal her shame. Anna was fed and cleaned, and that was about all. She was never carried, never encouraged to walk, never sung to or talked to, never cuddled and caressed. She was kept alive but deprived of all the loving care and training that make us distinctly human.

And what was the result?

After some hasty flipping of pages, the students reported on Anna. She could not walk. She could not speak. She could not dress herself. She was fearful of human beings. She was like Harlow's isolated baby monkeys.

To love, you must have been loved.

Before we check our scale with where we think human beings belong, someone nowadays will bring up the notion of abusive parents. They do not love because they were abused as children instead of loved. A cycle of abuse generates a cycle of abuse. Human beings can seek sexual gratification without loving their partners or the children that may result.

*   *   *

It would be quite unfair to leave the impression that all human behavior is learned. Some smart student usually brings up the recent twin studies by Thomas Bouchard at the University of Minnesota, which revealed some astonishing parallels in separated twins. Most of those parallels, however, showed up in physical traits, such as life span or a need to wear eyeglasses.

Encourage students to bring in data that conflict with the text or the teacher. Or that support them. But the conflict is always

more fun. And the teacher must always be wary of the risk of load-
ing the data one-sidedly.

So, then, what is the nature of human nature? You will have
some delightful class discussions in trying to reach an agreement on
that. However, ultimate agreement is not really the teacher's goal.
What you are really teaching is the process of testing ideas against
observation, theories against facts. It is also the discovery of the
assumptions that we make about human nature.

*   *   *

Discovering our assumptions about race deserves its own
chapter.

8

Discovering More Assumptions: Race

We are still working on the beliefs hidden inside our heads that bias our thinking without our knowing it. We need such beliefs and patterns for thinking. But we need patterns that correspond as closely as possible to the outside world of reality. Changing such patterns can be done best by experiential teaching, teaching by inquiry.

You start the class by handing a dictionary to a student, who reads aloud all the meanings of the word *white*. Another student writes the list on the blackboard, but selects only the metaphorical meanings, such as:

white	Free from spot or blemish
white	Free from moral impurity
white	Innocent
white	Marked by upright fairness
white	Not intended to cause harm
white	Favorable
white	Fortunate
white	Conservative or reactionary

Then switch to the metaphorical meanings of the word *black,* such as:

black	Thoroughly evil
black	Wicked
black	Soiled
black	Dirty
black	Invoking the devil
black	Gloomy
black	Calamitous
black	Sullen
black	Hostile

Sit back and wait. Don't ask any leading questions. Don't ask any questions at all. The class will boil over with comments.

Then, still using the dictionary, list the phrases beginning with *white*. The list will look much like this:

white book
white collar
whited sepulcher
white elephant
white feather
white flag
white friar
white house
white hunter
white lie
white livered
white man's burden
white plague
white primary
white slave
whitewash

Then repeat with phrases beginning with *black*. Omit the purely descriptive.

blackball
Blackbeard
black belt

    black bile
    black book
    black damp
    Black Death
    black dog
    black eye
    black flag
    Black Friday
    blackguard
    blackhead
    black-hearted
    Blackjack
    blackleg
    black-letter day
    blacklist
    black magic
    blackmail
    black market

The list goes on as far as black widow spider.

Once again, you need ask no questions. Wait. Listen. The comments will begin long before the list is finished. The class will teach themselves some simple semantics.

Some perceptive students will ask about other color terms used for race: red or yellow. Tell them to look in the dictionary and then tell the class. That will clinch it. They will begin to glimpse the effect on our thinking, the unconscious effect on our thinking, of the very language we use every day.

Underlying much race prejudice are subsidiary beliefs that support that prejudice. White people who believe blacks or Mexicans or Vietnamese to be inferior will say that they are stupid or immoral or lazy or list a whole set of character traits or mental traits.

How can the teacher modify the beliefs at the bottom before attempting to deal with the surface notions?

My assumption is that if you can provide students with accurate data, you can more easily shift some intolerance or change some prejudice. The assumption also is that avoiding intolerance is one of the goals of a class. Both of these I assume; I shall not bother to argue either. Prejudice is not easy to modify. These lessons won't do much; but we start with facts.

And we set a tone as to what attitudes are permissible in class; bigotry against other groups is one that the students can all easily become sensitized to and they all can avoid. If they cannot avoid bigotry, they can learn not to show it. That is the same argument as that laws can stop behavior that is discriminatory. Laws cannot, by themselves, stop prejudice, but without the discrimination, the prejudice does not flourish so abundantly.

"Hypocrisy," said La Rochefoucauld, "is the tribute which vice pays to virtue." Let the class decide what that means.

Let's start with gathering data on ability and setting up our list of materials. We need IQ scores for many different groups. We need to know how the scores were gathered and what kind of test was used. And we should have the range, the mean, the mode, the median, and various other such scores. Here is one way to do it.

In World War I (for you youngsters, that is the big European war that lasted from 1914 to 1918 and that the United States entered in 1917), the U.S. Army planned with Dr. Edward Thorndike to give a series of intelligence tests to draftees. The tests would help decide which men would be commissioned as officers. Millions of men were tested on a paper-and-pencil test, the Alpha test. Illiterates were given an oral test, the Beta. The tests were administered very unevenly and rather sloppily, according to Stephen Jay Gould (1981), who wrote a book called *The Mismeasure of Man*.

After World War I, this enormous volume of test scores was made available to psychologists for study. They immediately found that the average score for white soldiers was higher than the average score for Negro soldiers. In each state, the average (median) score for white men was higher. Next, much study and effort went into exploring why the Negro brain was so inferior, why the Negro could not learn. And these average scores provided official government proof that segregation of Negroes and whites was a good thing and should be continued.

After about ten years, one researcher made a disturbing discovery. You can discover it yourself by studying that table on the next page. It is right there in front of you. Some classes take thirty minutes; some take thirty seconds. Look again.

	Median Alpha Scores	
	White Men	Negro Men
Ohio	62.2	45.5
New York	53.8	38.6
Indiana	55.9	41.5
Illinois	61.6	42.2
Arkansas	35.6	16.1
Louisiana	36.1	13.4
Mississippi	37.6	10.3
Alabama	41.3	19.9

In a small pamphlet on *The Races of Mankind,* Dr. Ruth Benedict and Gene Weltfish (1943) told the story. But I would just put the figures in front of a class and let them discover for themselves. With the figures in this simple format, they could see it almost every time.

Can you? The hypothesis is that white men score higher than Negro men on the average. And most who read that statement read into it the meaning that any white man is smarter than any black man. Does the chart show either of those statements to be supported? Does the chart show that in every place? Look back and test that hypothesis. Are white men on the average earning higher scores than Negroes on the average? Everywhere?

Even in classes in the presumably enlightened sixties and seventies, I found many students who firmly resisted reading the chart on the angle: They would wriggle and squirm all around to find any reason why the statement that New York Negroes scored higher than Arkansas whites was inaccurate. Any reason would do.

If students in Minnesota felt that way, think how that discovery must have walloped a white southerner back in 1927. They wriggled and squirmed all over trying to find a rational answer. One first response was that all the smart Negroes had moved north. On second thought, most white southerners rejected this as too self-incriminating, but it was published in respectable journals, and Otto Klineberg, professor of psychology at the Sorbonne in Paris, did several careful studies to disprove it.

Of course, before we got to this point, the class had learned some simple statistical devices, such as mean, median, mode, and the simple frequency tables required to produce them.

After this, they would read some critical comments on the nature of intelligence testing and the problems inherent in using them incorrectly and the ways in which American schools have worshiped them as a key to all educational problems. One of the best books on the general subject of intelligence testing and race and culture is that of Stephen Jay Gould, who has written a column for *Natural History* for many years. *The Mismeasure of Man* examines all the basic ways in which whites have tried to prove the inferiority of all other peoples. Another is Howard Gardner's (1983) *The Frames of Mind*, which dissects intelligence into seven different abilities.

Still another is *The IQ Cult*, by Evelyn Sharp (1972), which tells about how American schools have overemphasized IQ scores and underemphasized the fact that the tests fail utterly to measure the person who has not had the same schooling as those who wrote the test.

Consider this test question. A picture is presented to a child, who is then asked, "What is missing from the picture?" The picture is of two stick figures, holding what most of us quickly recognize as tennis racquets. They are standing on a marked court with a tennis net between them. Show this to our kids, and most of them who have seen tennis courts can tell quickly that there is no tennis ball. Show it to some Salish Indian kids who have never seen a tennis court in their lives but whose survival centers around the annual salmon run upstream, and they might stare at it for a while and then ask where the salmon are. What they see are fishnets and dip nets. The Salish kids flunk that test question and many others that are based on cultural knowledge. Therefore, they earn low IQ scores.

Let's pull a switch. Adrian Dove developed a "Counter-Intelligence Test" in which the questions were based on the sort of things that black ghetto kids might learn. To pass it, you must know terms such as *blood, short-dog, Mother's Day, Handkerchief Head, Uncle Tom, Oreo, Juneteenth, Hambone, the man,* and a host of others, few of which mean what they seem to mean to the WASPs. When my color-blind friend Bill Polich administered this test to his sociology classes, the black students got higher scores than the white students, but they still missed plenty. They complained that the test was outdated, that slang changed too fast. Also, few of them came from the Watts ghetto where Adrian Dove was a social worker.

What do intelligence tests measure?

Theodora Kroeber (1979), the author of *Ishi,* wrote an account of the last surviving member of a California tribe of Indians whose relatives had all been hunted down and killed by sheriff's posses who used to spend weekends on a party shooting Indians for sport. If you take the Bay Area Rapid Transit (BART) from San Francisco under the bay to Berkeley and farther east to Walnut Creek, you will see Mount Diablo, where Ishi tried to hide from the killers of his people.

Ishi managed to survive and to make some friends and ended up teaching the professional anthropologists how to live in the wilderness, starting from scratch. One summer, he in effect challenged the white anthropologists to go into the woods, leave behind all knives and tools, strip naked, and then survive. Instead, they went along just to photograph and to learn. Ishi showed them how it was done. He quickly chipped a sharp stone and then soon made some string from bark. With the string, he set rabbit snares. Then he made more string, constructed a spear and a bow, and built a fire. With his snares he caught rabbits, which he skinned and cooked and ate, keeping the skins for clothing. He soon had a survival kit and a survival camp in operation.

I could have done the same thing had I been taught how since I was a kid. Certainly. And so could Ishi have learned how to adjust the gears on a ten-speed bicycle had he been taught. And many of us can still learn at any age—unless we are held back by the discrimination of the dominant group, unless the prejudice against us is so strong that we cannot learn, cannot go to school, cannot get a decent job.

Students who read Dee Brown's (1970) *Bury My Heart at Wounded Knee* learned how the different tribes of Native Americans lost their land, then were cheated of their miserable payments for the land, and then were blamed for being poor and shiftless. We like to blame the victim. Those who did not read Dee Brown did not believe what other students told them. Most of our learning is incremental, a bit at a time. And our insights are personal. We cannot gain another's insight.

*   *   *

Can they learn? Can people from fairly primitive cultures actually learn to cope with modern civilization?

Or perhaps we should rephrase that to ask whether we can learn that other human beings have the same abilities that we do. Experiential learning using inquiry, discovery, and induction will make the most effective changes in our mental blocks.

When the Australian soldiers were fighting the Japanese troops invading northern Australia in 1942, they were desperately short of manpower. The troops would travel by truck across the great desert of central Australia, and in so doing they frequently made friends with the aborigines, especially the children.

Boys hung around the camps. They loved to ride in the trucks, and they enjoyed learning to change tires and then learning to change oil and grease. Children whose parents used stone knives jumped almost instantly into handling modern machinery. They learned to repair vehicles, to drive them, to service them, to become mechanics. From the Stone Age to the Machine Age in one leap.

J. J. Rohrer, a researcher from the University of Oklahoma, tested a number of groups of American Indians for IQ. On the Goodenough Draw-a-Man Test, the Osage Indian children scored higher than the white children. Then he used a language test, and again the Osage scored higher than the whites. The Osage reservation was on land where oil had been discovered; the Osage were wealthy and had good schools. The poor Indians had poor schools, with the result that their IQ scores were low.

Another researcher, T. R. Garth, of the University of Denver, in 1935 published a study on intelligence testing of Indians. The average score was 81. But Indian children who had been adopted by white families averaged 102, while their siblings left on the reservation scored only 87 on the average.

When you present such data to a class, don't ask leading questions. Just ask for comments. The students will soon enough decide that the intelligence tests measure how well one has learned the culture of the folks who wrote the test.

Those test writers were most often males. Ask the women in your classes to construct some tests on traditional female tasks and test the reaction of the class. Ask the farm kids to construct test questions.

How would you construct an intelligence test that was fair to people of other cultures? A culture-fair test? Or a culture-free test?

Ask that of any group at your next dinner party. But don't argue with their answers; others will challenge them quickly enough.

Some will want to use pictures only. Some will want to use numbers only. Some will want to use blocks and pegs and puzzles only.

Don't tell anyone that it hasn't been done yet.

*   *   *

Remember Ray Cloud, the Chippewa, who learned fast enough to catch an error on my chart? A month later that summer, I was talking to a white woman teacher in an Indian school who had referred to "stupid Indians." She had been teaching a Head Start class trying to prepare young kids for school.

"I get so exasperated with those children. They are so stupid. They don't even take help."

"What do you mean?"

She explained that she had been trying to get children ready for a reading-readiness test. They were to listen to a list of words and draw a circle around the picture of the thing listed.

"The first row had three animals. A giraffe, an elephant, and a walrus. I told them to draw a circle around the giraffe. None of them knew which was a giraffe. They're just plain stupid."

"Well, I suppose that they had never seen a giraffe."

"That's no excuse. Most kids have never seen a giraffe, but they know what one is."

Now one trick in interviewing someone is never to argue, just look pleasant and get them talking and grunt amiably every so often. So I did not bring up what it was like for a child to grow up in a one-room house with no books, no newspapers, no magazines, and with parents who had never seen a giraffe. Instead, I grunted amiably.

"What other questions did the test have?"

"Another one I remember was the difference between a staircase, an elevator, and an escalator. They messed up on that one, too."

"How would you teach them the difference?"

"Well, I did right then. I told them that a staircase was inside a house. That an elevator was a big box that went up and down in a big building and an escalator was a moving staircase that they could see in big stores in Minneapolis. Then it turned out that they didn't know where Minneapolis was or even what it was. So I tried to show them how to figure out by elimination. If they were sure that one answer was wrong, they could guess at the other two and get it right half the time."

"And did they understand that?"

"Not a word. Some of them still don't know when to guess on a test. If they don't know the answer, they leave it blank. They're stupid."

Or maybe honest, I thought.

That same evening, I learned that she had taught on the reservation for several years. She had never visited the home of a single child. She did not understand cultural differences or cultural deprivation. Her contempt for the Chippewa glowered through all her speech. They were stupid children who did not appreciate all that she did for them. They would grow up to be as bad as their parents.

By listening only, I managed to learn a lot. But not once did I attempt to teach her how wrong she was. My role that evening was that of collector. And I knew my limitations.

The younger teachers were much better.

*   *   *

A team of psychologists in New York once tried to determine the attitudes of young black children toward being black. K. and M. Clark constructed an experiment in which they interviewed young black children one at a time. While waiting for the interview, the children played with several dolls, some with white skin, some with dark skin.

The interview included several questions about the dolls.

A. "Give me the doll you like to play with."
B. "Give me the doll that is nice."
C. "Give me the doll that looks bad."
D. "Give me the doll that is a nice color."

When I told a class about this experiment, I usually stopped at that point. I told them that responses of the kids came in three columns: the colored doll, the white doll, and "don't know." Instead of telling the class the results, I first asked them to anticipate, to guess what the pattern of answers would be by putting in a percentage for each column. And to write down a reason for their guess. The reason constituted the theory behind the guess. Only after they had all written down their guesses would I show them the Clarks' actual findings. Let me repeat that caveat: Make them write down their guesses and state their assumptions about the reason.

Here are the data:

	Colored Doll	White Doll	Don't Know
A.	32	61	1
B.	38	59	3
C.	59	17	24
D.	38	60	2

And, once more, I would try to keep my mouth shut. Just let the class compare their guesses with the actual responses and then try to determine what it meant. Wait.

They never failed me. Since we had earlier learned about concepts of self-image and socialization and feelings of self-worth, they had the intellectual tools to cope with the data. Any assumptions that the kids had just fallen into a pattern of answers were erased by question C, where the reversal took place. Some students would have tears in their eyes when they grasped the insight of what self-hatred can do to the self-image and the self-esteem of a child.

This experiment by the Clarks was introduced into the 1954

Supreme Court case of *Brown* v. *Board of Education,* which resulted
in the orders to desegregate schools. The old argument had been for
"separate but equal" schools. Now the Court held that separate
schools could not be equal. The counterargument by the segrega-
tionists was that social science experiments had no relevance to a
court case or to the question of constitutionality. Only legal terms
could be used.

That also leads to a class discussion on trying to define *equal*
without using any psychological measure or sociological measure
or economic measure.

Many students read Alex Haley's (1965) first well-known
book, *The Autobiography of Malcolm X,* and came across Malcolm's attempts to induce pride among blacks by a rejection of hair
straighteners and bleaches and such attempts at copying the appearance of white people. Suddenly this campaign took on new
meaning.

And why did the expression "Black is beautiful" appear suddenly in the 1960s?

Frequently a white student will burst out in irritation with
"Blacks are racist too, so it comes out even." This leads to a discussion of *even,* which often echoes those discussions over *equality.*

*   *   *

Writing should play a major part in all of this learning.
Writing a report on a book was greatly encouraged by bonus points
added to the final grade. The form of the report, however, was a
rather rigid one which I swiped from Mortimer Adler's (1972) *How
to Read a Book.* Adler swiped it from Aristotle. Simply put, the
critic should answer three questions:

What was the author trying to do?
How well did the author do it?
Was it worth doing?

But I found that after years of writing summaries as reports on
books, most students still wrote summaries. So I added a requirement to write a page of summary and then do the analysis. To save
my time, I usually skipped reading the summaries.

* * *

As I write this chapter in May of 1989 in Minnesota, the Chippewa Indians in Wisconsin are spearing fish at night using lights. A great many white fishermen and resort owners are responding with rage, jeers, rocks, and placards with slogans such as "Save a Walleye, Spear an Indian."

When the Chippewa signed a treaty in 1837 giving away most of their lands, they kept the right to hunt and fish and gather wild rice on the lands given up. The white men ignored this treaty right until the Indians finally won it back in a court battle in 1983 with white lawyers before white judges.

In Minnesota, almost the same thing happened. However, Minnesota dickered with the tribes and bought off their rights, paying the Chippewa several million dollars each year. But Wisconsin refused. In both states, hundreds of resort owners earn their living by renting cabins to tourists who come to fish for walleyes. Many of them are now demanding that the treaties be abrogated and the Indians be kept on the reservations. In May of 1989, hundreds of jeering and swearing white folks gathered at the docks to try to stop the Indians. When the whites began throwing rocks, the sheriffs arrested many.

The governor of the state first made a deal with the Indians. "You limit your spearfishing and we will protect you."

But when the protests continued and the deputy sheriffs became exhausted, the governor told the Indians that he could no longer protect them and ordered them to quit spearing. His critics pointed out that when a mob threatens lives, the governor's duty is to protect the victim, not the mob.

And then a curious thing happened. About a thousand supporters of the Indians rallied in the state capital to protest the governor's backing down. They held up placards with slogans such as "Support Rights, Not Racists."

It is a clash between two economies and two races and two cultures. It may well happen again next year.

Were I still teaching, I would love to use this example. Think of all the hidden assumptions, the stereotypes, the ignorance of history, the culture conflict, the feeling of victimization on both sides, the marvelous opportunities for teaching, the marvelous opportunity for stretching minds, for rebuilding mental patterns more consonant with the world of reality.

However, such a teaching opportunity also creates a risk of classroom propagandizing. Keep open your requests for more data, more background information, more history. Be on guard against taking one side. The proper role of the teacher is to get students to learn how to think critically, how to question those hidden assumptions. Let them discover.

*   *   *

Dick Flores, a Chiricahua Apache, pointed out to me once that the young Southeast Asian students were winning many high school scholarships. "You've gotta watch out for those boat people. We Indians were helpful to some boat people once, and they swiped our whole country."

*   *   *

An applicant to teach in our college sat across from my desk and told me how he had lived in Phoenix for several years and spent a lot of time visiting Indians on the reservation.

"Which reservation was this?"

"Oh, gosh, the name escapes me."

"Was it a big one north of Phoenix?" I thought that he might have meant the Navajo.

"No, it was west, I think."

Suddenly I had a nasty thought. Innocently I asked him, "Could it be the Anasazi?" (The Anasazi, the ancient predecessors of the Hopi and Zuni, have been gone for many centuries.)

"Yes, of course. Now I remember." And he launched into a long description of his many visits to a chief of the Anasazi, using nothing but Hollywood clichés and stereotypes to describe the Indians.

We did not hire him.

9

Clear Writing
Makes
Clear Thinking

Most of us think that the important part of an experiment in school is getting the right answer or remembering that answer. Here I'm proposing that more important is knowing how a theory works and how to construct an experiment to test a theory.

Writing is an important step in learning how to think clearly. When you commit your speculation to paper, you cannot fudge it later by faulty memory. Write it down.

As teacher, you do not have time to check your students' notebooks for grammar and spelling and clarity. No, but you can ask students to read each other's notes when it comes to writing down a theory. Students can be far more effective critics than most of us teachers can be. And far more ruthless. Moreover, we all listen to our peers.

In a class discussion of the Clarks' experiment described in Chapter Eight, one student proposed as a reason why a black chi'd would select a particular doll "whether or not you like a color." The student sitting next to him rumbled, "That's just nonsense. It's not just color. It's the color of the kid that counts."

History teachers traditionally ask students to read collections of source material, documents of the period. And they usually ask students to write notes. Usually we don't instruct very much in that skill.

Try this assignment: "Write a précis for each document you read. A précis is a brief summary maintaining the author's point of view, maintaining the author's meaning, and maintaining the author's tone. Usually it is short: one paragraph or one page."

With a lot of practice, they can do it. With a little practice and some classroom comparisons, they can do it much more quickly.

The concern here is not to embarrass students who are struggling to learn. So make transparencies of student précis for purposes of comparison and criticism. But take them from another section or a previous year, and never reveal the name of the writer. Show them on the screen. Don't say a word. Let the students decide whether that writer had summarized the whole document and maintained the original point of view, the original meaning, and the original tone.

Very quickly they call out the violations.

"It seems to me."

"This writer is trying to say."

"His tone was pretty dull."

"The writer contradicted herself."

And once again, the group teaches itself that none of those comments maintains the original point of view. Once the class grasps more clearly what to do, you give them a chance to modify their papers and to compare with those of their neighbors. Peer-group criticism is very effective.

But if the author did contradict herself, the student wants to remember that. Show it in the précis. Fine. Or put that in a separate note at the bottom of the page. Or use red ink to show where. Just don't confuse your comment with the précis.

The point of writing précis is to learn careful reading and careful writing and keeping your opinion out of it.

*   *   *

"But don't I even get credit for trying?" The student clutched his paper, staring at the two pages he had written and at the grade of zero. "Look how much I wrote. I wrote lots more than most of the class did."

The poor child had wangled his way past some exhausted

teachers for years by the device of filling up page after page. Then he ran into a teacher who read it, read it again, and failed to find anything significant or relevant in it. It was guff, fluff, snow, or some ruder expression. It was not an answer to the question, or to any question.

How can you teach students to distinguish between clear answers and snow jobs?

They need to compare the two; they need to see them side by side. I did not invent that. My writing teacher at the University of Oklahoma, Walter Campbell, used it on me, and I doubt that he invented it. Campbell is better known as Stanley Vestal, a pen name under which he produced novels, poetry, histories, and short stories adding up to about twenty books.

He told us what to look for in clear writing and then gave us four or five different passages and asked us to rank them and tell why.

It sounds simple until you try to rank them and tell why.

Like most teachers, when I discovered someone using a good method, I swiped it. I gave my students copies of the brief test essays shown below, which I had taken from another sociology class, and asked them to rank them from best to worst. All of the essays answered the same question: "Define the term *Ethnocentrism* and give three examples. Relate your examples back to the definition. Use the language of sociology in writing."

And you, reader, do it as well. Pick out the best. Pick out the worst. Then rank the others in between. While you are doing it, you can also sharpen your understanding of ethnocentrism.

The students were also to score each one on the basis of ten points: four points for a clear, workable definition and two points for each clearly developed example. I scored their papers that way; they might as well learn what was important to me.

Score Each Answer and Defend Your Choice:

A. Ethnocentrism is the belief that one's own way or society is superior to all others. We Americans tend to clump all those who do not speak English as foreigners. This is one example of ethnocentrism. There are

many other examples of ethnocentrism. Other in-
stances of thinking, for instance, that our neighbor-
hood is better than another or that our American
society is more advanced than others.

B. Ethnocentrism is the feeling that one's own group,
nation, or race is the best. A good example of ethnocentrism from the Readings is the study of the zoot-
suiters in California. In this paper, the zoot-suiters,
who were usually Mexicans, were fighting with the
sailors in the area. The zoot-suiters thought that they
were the best and the sailors thought that they were
the best. Ethnocentrism is commonly associated with
in-groups and out-groups because of the feelings of
the in-groups which in this case were the sailors.
Another good example is the feeling of the Black Mus-
lims that the dark-colored people are much superior
to the white.

C. Ethnocentrism is the feeling by a person in a society that their culture, their norms, their ideas and
ways of life are the best way for people to live and to
believe.

    In class we pondered the question: "Is it wrong
for a mother to deliberately kill her baby?" We all said
"Yes." That another society might not think this mor-
ally wrong never occurred to us until we heard the
story of the aboriginal mother in the desert. She could
scarcely find enough food for herself and her three-
year old. With the baby along, all three might die. Her
society told her to kill the newly born child in order
to save the older one. But we still think that our way
is better.

    Another example would be the missionaries in
Hawaii who made the natives believe in God.

    Or the Mormons and the homesteaders who
didn't like each other. Each thought their way was
best.

The eating habits of different people is another case. We think that eating beetles and worms and blubber is dirty and disgusting and unhealthy. We sneer at hungry people who have learned to eat the food available. They might be disgusted at our eating bloody steaks or sardine intestines or raw oysters.

D. Ethnocentrism is an important concept in any attempt at making a sociological analysis or in reading or understanding any of the relevant studies in this field. Ethnocentrism certainly stands out as one of the more basic philosophical attitudes which every student must master if he wishes to cope with the complexities and the philosophical subtleties of sociology. Many students ignore this very basic idea and confuse it with a vague and compassionate approach to problems when they should be examining it under the subsidiary concepts relevant to ethnocentrism. One cannot stress too much the importance and the inevitability of using a concept so basic to the whole important field of sociology. Any sociologist will not only agree with this, he or she will confirm it wholeheartedly and with more adequate footnotes than I could possibly bring to bear upon this great topic in such a limited format as a brief essay in class under time pressure. Be that as it may, ethnocentrism is crucial; it is key; it is dominant; and we all must understand this central place in the realm of sociological analysis. Had I more time I would be happy to expound upon the manifold realms of analysis which would be open to the keen student once he masters this key concept, so elemental, so basic to our understanding. Without it we would be unable to grasp the greater nuances and the subtler insights which come to those who have thoroughly and completely mastered this analytical tool.

Did you rank each and then score each? Don't read any farther until you have scored the four samples. I mean that. Go back and do it. You read my book, you play my game.

*   *   *

No contest, apparently. Example C won easily. Many of the students gave it a perfect score. But not all. And the real discussion arose when we began to analyze each one separately.

Did they define the concept in terms of a belief about cultural superiority? Or did they confuse it with racism? Did they use such terms as *norms, mores, folkways, artifacts, values, beliefs,* to indicate that they knew what culture included? Did the examples clearly show how someone felt about his or her own culture as compared to another culture?

After we had discussed the essays, I graded them. Most of the students had been very generous.

Example A gained one point for a partial definition that did not even mention the term *culture,* or *norms,* or *folkways,* or *mores,* or anything like that. The first example is not appropriate; *foreigners* is not a derogatory term in itself. From there on, the essay is just gaseous repetition. Total: one point out of ten.

Example B. The definition is confused with racism; it clarifies nothing. The zoot-suiter example came close to the mark, for only one point. The second example is of racism and is not developed. Total: one point out of ten.

Example C. Definition clear: four points. First example very descriptive and clearly appropriate: two points. Second example almost okay but not saying "our god" or "the missionaries' god" reveals that the writer did not recognize his own ethnocentrism. One point. Third example unclear: no points. Fourth example very good: two points. Total: 9 points out of ten.

Example D. No definition. No examples. Pure, unadulterated guff. But this sometimes works. I know two students who got through college writing stuff almost like this. They wrote so many pages that some tired teachers just glanced at them and marked a C. Total: zero out of ten.

The shock waves were visible. Many clearly expected at least a score of five, or 50 percent, for putting down *some* words, for "trying." Worst were the wordy mush-slingers who thought that example D was the best. Several actually rated it as worth ten points. They were the talkative ones who had learned to fill the air with meaningless jargon. Often they ended their sentences with "or something." Yet when challenged to read aloud the definition or an example, they could not find any.

A radio disc jockey in one of my classes where this type of writing discipline was maintained just quit the class. He told me that I was ruining his professional life by insisting on facts. He had to be able to fill the gaps between records by saying nothing that sounded like something, or something like, you know, something. Or whatever. Basically, you know, he had to talk, like the man said.

The use of transparencies for displaying student writing is a great tool. We all need models, muddy and clear models, logical, illogical, organized, and disorganized models, and we need to learn to distinguish between them.

Let them discover the distinctions.

Then let them defend their discoveries.

Used with care, a transparency will also display some of the handwriting that a teacher is expected to disentangle and decode. Just make sure that the student's name is not showing. Better to use examples from the year before or from another section of the class.

As for the really bad handwriting, you can borrow one simple technique. The student got no grade. The paper came back with a question mark in the corner. Usually he would rush up (most often it was a he) saying, "You didn't give me a grade."

"Well, I couldn't read your writing."

"You mean I don't get any grade at all?"

"Oh sure, you do. Just copy it neatly and turn both papers in right now."

In about three minutes, he would turn in a neatly written page, which might or might not get a good grade. Except for the few with real physical difficulties, most of us can write far more legibly than we do write. I know that I can.

*   *   *

Another method, best for the early days of a class, is to assign a brief essay as a quiz and then ask students to exchange their essays with each other and criticize the way they are handled. Some are utterly baffled at first, but they learn to look for structure and clarity and relevance. This process takes time and explanation. It pays off in much clearer answers and much better grades.

I used a variation on this for students' reports on books or on short research papers. Each report had to be signed by another student, indicating that he or she had read it for clear writing, correct spelling, and conventional grammar. The student who proofread such a paper earned a bonus in the grade book; the student who selected some buddy who knew no better than he or she did had to do it over again and on second try would pick a better proofreader.

This preliminary screening permits the teacher to process a large volume of paper, knowing that the stuff coming in is at least readable and has passed muster with another reader.

*   *   *

One very ineffectual student, barely able to write two coherent sentences, turned in three book reports, beautifully written and neatly typed.

I called Doug to my office. "You must really have enjoyed this book. How did you like those rather difficult opening chapters? And what made you keep on reading despite that?"

He mumbled with his head down. Obviously, he had never read the book and knew nothing about it.

When I repeated this with the second book, poor Doug twisted his hands and kept his head down. When I asked him where he had learned to type, he confessed. His girlfriend had written all three of the reports. I was pretty sure, because she had turned in three excellent reports for herself on three other books. Busy girl. Smart, too.

The girlfriend came in, shy and scared. We went over the ethics of cheating for someone else, and she obviously felt pretty abashed about her behavior. But she didn't expect to hear what I did say to her.

"These three reports get torn up because Doug did not do them. And your reports as well, because you cheated for him.

"Now let me tell you two other things. First, if you keep up the work you are doing, you will earn an A in this class without any book reports. You don't need them.

"Now for the other thing. You can do a lot better in picking boyfriends. Don't underrate yourself."

She stared at me. She blushed. She giggled. She started to cry through her giggles. And then she grabbed some Kleenex off my desk and mopped her eyes. As she left, I repeated: "Don't underrate yourself."

A few weeks later, I saw her with a young man that I would have rated her match.

* * *

Students also need help in organizing an essay when writing a test. One way to do it, particularly when under time pressure, is the pyramid style, the structure used in many newspaper articles. Give examples of these to your students; let them analyze the structure to find out which is which.

The pyramid format squeezes the whole story into one opening sentence complete with names and dates and places and some conclusion as to why and how.

Then the second paragraph expands on the names, identifying them more completely, and expands on another point, telling more about that.

The third paragraph expands on when and why the event happened.

The fourth paragraph expands on how it happened.

The fifth may range more widely afield, bringing in quotations from another source.

The sixth may tie in a related story.

The seventh ranges more widely.

As you add each paragraph, you add less and less important material. The newspaper editor cuts off the bottom end to fit the space. You cut off the bottom end to fit the time.

The key to this pyramid device is to pack everything of major significance clearly into the first paragraph. Make it clear, make it factual, make it relevant.

If you still have time, you can add another paragraph to show that you really knew a lot more and would love to tell it. But be sure to add. Some just rehash the first paragraph three or four times and think that they have followed the pyramid style.

This is about the best format for students who must write several essays under time pressure. But to do it well, you must jot down phrases in an outline to guide you. Jot them down in the margin and rearrange till they make the most sense.

More impressive, if you have the time to write it, is the reverse approach. Here you give all the facts first, building paragraph on paragraph. Then, at the end, you state your conclusion, which is the final answer to the question. This approach brings the reader along with you, convincing that reader of the logical conclusion before you state it. I sure hope that this sounds familiar to you by now. And to do this well, you must really outline in advance by jotting down a few phrases in an outline.

Students need help in learning how to handle tests and the pressure of testing. Look in Chapter Fourteen, on the role of the teacher, for some comments on stress. And remember Betty with her fossil amulet in Chapter Five.

*   *   *

Whenever you write a set of test questions, take a quick peek at Benjamin Bloom's (1956) very, very helpful *Taxonomy of Educational Objectives*. His classification gives you a fast review of which items can be tested well in objective tests, such as terms, specific facts, conventions, trends, sequences, criteria, methodology.

For more complex questions, ask for brief essays on universals, abstractions, principles, organizations, theories, and structures.

So much for memory stuff. What really counts is how to test students' comprehension by means of translating, interpreting, extrapolating, and applying. Most of this is better done with essays.

On a higher level yet is testing the ability to analyze relationships and principles.

Even more demanding, says Bloom, is the synthesizing of separate elements into a whole.

And toughest of all is evaluating, making a judgment by analyzing internal evidence or comparing with external measuring devices.

Bloom's book gives clear examples for testing every kind and level of knowledge. If you don't have a copy on your desk now, buy one.

*   *   *

The encyclopedia salesman was showing his wares to an audience of two who had invited him in.

But he queered his pitch.

"We also have these coupons. Each one is redeemable for extra research on some topic that you may be interested in and need the most modern facts about. All you need do is to tell us what you need and send in one of these coupons, and our experts will mail you a written report. Students find it very helpful for term papers." And he smirked.

The rest of that scene I shall not describe.

I had known for years of a black market in term papers for college students and had already worked out my answer to it. It was the one-page term paper.

The paper was filled with all the mechanics. But since it was going to be short, it did not panic the freshmen. And since it was short, I could easily check every step of the way, even with a fairly large class.

In history classes, I would list a number of historical events, let them select one, and bring in a bibliography of books and articles on it. Check by the instructor. Go on and read them and make notes. Bring me your notes. Check. Now outline what you plan to write. Check. Now write it in about three pages in your own words. Include the footnotes. Check. Now cut it to one page, still in your own words. Now write it neatly and add a page of footnotes and a page of bibliography. By that time, the student had ten facts for every sentence and was forced to select and choose the most effective parts to present.

How different from the padding and copying that most of them had done before. With this format, we usually managed a brief paper each quarter. They got easier and easier to write.

*   *   *

When students first read about other cultures in some depth, they daydream about going to Samoa or Kenya or Madagascar, where they will live among the natives, learn the language, and record for posterity their keen and brilliant observations on the food, the tools, the clothing, the housing, the world view, and, of course, the sex life of the natives.

Few can ever manage it. But we can work out a substitute learning experience of stepping into another culture, of struggling with a slightly different language, and of looking at the world through different eyes. The trick lies in looking at a local subculture, yes, one right here in River City, where views and language and beliefs are just different enough to make their study fascinating.

Some titles from ethnographic papers my students have written:

"A Paper Boy"
"Kindergarten"
"A Formal Wear Distributor"
"A Waitress"
"Massage Parlor"
"Truck Driver"
"Carpet Salesman"
"TV Photographer"
"Marijuana Dealer"
"Winnebago Grandpa"
"Bowhunter"
"Root-Beer Drive-In Car-Hop"
"YMCA Game Room"
"Prison Maximum Security Unit"
"Seventh Grader"
"Shelter for Homeless"
"Cab Driver"
"Child's View of Babysitters"
"TV Repairman"
"Harness Racers"

"Cheerleader"
"Dog-Sled Racer"

Our models came originally from a provocative little book, *The Cultural Experience: Ethnography in Complex Society,* by James P. Spradley and David W. McCurdy (1972). As more and more students did their fieldwork and discovered their taxonomies and wrote up their papers, I built up a local collection of papers that enormously reassured the timid that this could actually be done by freshmen.

Spradley and McCurdy taught them how to ask questions and how to see the world through the eyes of the informant. We practiced in class questioning each other and informants who were brought in. Interviewing is not easy, but it is very rewarding and one of the finest methods for dealing with your own ethnocentrism.

The easiest subcultures to study are those in which the informants interact with each other and develop a private language that they use to deal with the world. Truck drivers and cab drivers and waitresses and dog racers and horse racers and hunters all have a lingo apart from the rest of us. And the slang or the terms they use are often the keys to revealing how such people look at the world.

*   *   *

Some cases:
One young woman talked with prisoners in a maximum-security lockup. Here is one of her taxonomies on three types of people as seen by prisoners:

1. Pigs, screws, and guards made up the first category.
2. Cons made up the second. Good cons might be dope freaks, mellow types, don't bug you, won't trick you, can be respected, and are up front.

   Bad cons included freako rapists, straights who turn into snitches, and the snitches who get in favor with the pigs by snitching on you.
3. Visitors including relatives, lawyers, pigs, and do-gooders.

Another student interviewed a seventh-grader and found this view of teachers:

There are two kinds of teachers: nice ones and mean ones.

Nice teachers are those who forget assignments, say please, ignore smoking, joke around like hell, goof around, keep the radio on, let kids talk, grade fair.

Mean teachers are those who are femmy, have pets, bad breath, think they are god's gift, mean, too personal, threatening, throw kids, throw chairs at kids, pound on kids, check pockets, check lockers.

One woman interviewed her son's friends to find out what they did in the game room of the local YMCA. She found a variety of activities:

Check the candy and pop machines for coins left in and for ripping off candy or pop.

Get into trouble: have bare feet, fool with the machines, break things, go behind desk, throw garbage around.

Play games: pay for yourself or watch others, take over games from little kids; rip off the machine.

Students who have worked through interviews and diagrammed the informant's world view, how the informant sees other people, gain a richer perspective on life. Those who enter the project with the ability to enjoy satire seem to get more out of it. Those who dare not venture far afield end up interviewing a close friend or a sibling. They learn very little.

My usual advice on selecting a topic was to pick one about which you knew nothing. Men might pick traditional women's roles, women pick traditional men's roles. One macho football player confessed modestly that he could not select a topic of which he was ignorant because he knew quite a lot about almost everything. The proposal of interviewing a woman made him terribly uneasy. So did the idea of interviewing an old man or a child.

Finally, without telling me, he selected football. He interviewed himself. He botched it completely. Since he flunked the tests also, that made no difference. Some people are not yet ready.

Those who are ready to learn from an ethnography are a joy. They are climbing up to stage seven or eight on Perry's scheme. They are beyond Dualism and often getting into Relativism. They are rebuilding their mental patterns; they are gaining in critical skills and acumen as well as knowledge. They are moving into the area of Commitment and maturing considerably as they do.

That is one reason why having adults return to college has been such a joy to teachers. Many of those students have struggled through these stages on their own. Those who have not are often aware that they need to recast some mental patterns.

*   *   *

One more writing technique: When I was interviewing other teachers for some examples of good teaching, I took notes. Then I wrote up a few pages of description to add to this book. They appear at the beginning of Chapter Twelve.

But then I hesitated. Suppose I had seriously misquoted one of those people?

Back I went with my printout to show it to them.

Sure enough. Errors. Gordon Meyers told me that it would be too risky to let students cut themselves to make blood sample slides. He did the cutting, the sampling, and the staining. Jerry Tammen changed the word *dye* to *reagent*. And he corrected the description of the test for coliform bacteria. Where I had written "percentages of solutions," he wrote it as "volumes."

When they had tidied up my prose, I mentioned that if I had been a news reporter working on a daily deadline, they would never have had this opportunity. They responded with stories of misquotations and misstatements that creep into the daily press and radio as well as into student papers.

Suddenly it occurred to me: What a device for having students learn how well they were interviewing, making notes, reconstructing notes, and writing from memory. Take it back to the guy you talked to. Let that one be your teacher and critic. You will never get a better.

This type of interviewing, collecting, analyzing, and writing ethnographies helps the student move into Piaget's fourth stage of thinking. Those who accept the challenge move up more readily on Perry's nine-point scale.

10

Discovering Rules: Cousins, Coins, and Rune Stones

On the screen flashed the title of the first slide in bold letters: "THE UNKNOWN LAND." A voice from the tape recorder spoke: "Several years ago I traveled to a dry and desert land that was strange and new to me. A young man who lived there talked to me about each of my photographs. Here is what the young man said."

First picture: canyon with red rock walls, a scraggly pine clinging to a crevice, jumbled red rocks lying on the ground.

Voice: "The mother of my mother lived for a year in this canyon. She was hiding from the soldiers. She lived in a cave. She ate nuts and roots and lizards and snakes and rats. Pretty tough. Lots of people died in those years. But the soldiers never did catch her."

Another slide: a flock of sheep in desert grass with a herdsman on horseback.

Voice: "These sheep belong to my mother. She has lots of sheep. She has about four hundred left even after losing many in the snowstorms last winter. Her mother had a brother who had lots of sheep. My father doesn't have many sheep. That's because his mother didn't have many brothers. They all died young."

Slide: a rock house built into a ledge in a steep red cliff that mounts in a sheer wall hundreds of feet above.

Voice: "I don't like this place. We never go near this place. The old ones used to live here, long ago in that house in the cliff. We call them the Anasazi. But I would like a piece of flint the old ones made. My mother's brother has a piece of flint from the old ones. He promised me that someday I would have it. There is real power in those old flint arrowheads."

Slide: an old, tumbledown house, eight-sided, made of logs and with the roof covered with dirt.

Voice: "I don't like that place. We never go near that place. My father's father died there two winters ago and I helped to bury him under a cliff. It was terrible. We killed both of his horses, too. I never go there. We turn aside long before we get there. His *tchindi* might still be there. You never can tell. I don't like to look at this picture."

The tape and slides went on, showing attitudes toward owls and wolves and kangaroo rats and snakes and cactus and agave and dead people and healing ceremonies and the beautiful desert itself. The young man, without explaining, had looped listeners into a mystery.

That was my final, published version. It was a good lesson. It still is. It always works.

But I did not start out that way.

My start was pretty awful. Several people told me so.

*   *   *

In the summer of 1967, I came to understand more clearly the method of inquiry teaching. The most thanks go to Ted Dethlefsen and Bob Spaulding.

Seven of us met in Airlie House Conference Center outside of Washington, D.C. As the writer of a curriculum in anthropology for junior high students for the Unitarian Universalist Association, I offered my opening lesson. The other six were advisers and critics.

That wretched lesson consisted of a set of slides and a taped lecture about them. The slides I had taken in Arizona around Canyon de Chelly and the Painted Desert, and they were pretty good photos.

For the first slide, of the red rocks in a steep canyon with some scraggly pine trees, I heard my voice saying, "These are red rocks in a steep canyon typical of this area. Notice the scraggly pine trees."

When I showed the slide of the horseman herding the sheep, I told my audience that it was a man on horseback herding some sheep.

The critics criticized.

"A travelogue."

"A monologue."

"A boring travelogue monologue. Try again."

What my critics said was not kind, but it was both true and necessary. They sent me back to the typewriter and tape recorder.

Later that day, Ted Dethlefsen suggested a format. "You might try another voice. Have a native respond to each picture. That way you can leap right into the culture and explore attitudes and responses and beliefs and background. And don't try to explain; leave that to the students to figure out."

That night, I brooded long. About four in the morning, I dressed, took my tape recorder, and composed a brand-new set of comments, using the culture of the Navajo.

Better. Far better. Day-from-night better. Ruth Underhill, our expert on Navajos, asked me to change a few sentences and suggested some additions. Ruth had just published her big book on *Red Man's Religion* (Underhill, 1965). She also had recently returned to the Navajo reservation for a Medicine Sing and had had an old Singer bless her and her valuable possessions. When I asked what her valuable possessions were, she said her eyeglasses, her wallet, and her car keys.

Instead of a dull travelogue for the slide show, I now had a mystery. Who is the speaker? Why does he talk about mother's brother and father's father? Why is he frightened of an abandoned house? What is *tchindi*? Why kill two horses? Why were those soldiers trying to kill an old woman? And who were the soldiers?

The problem was to answer as many questions as possible about the persons and the land in the slides and on the tape. What questions? Well, first you ask the class to figure out what questions they should ask. But I never had to ask any class to do that. They leap into asking questions. Who are these people? Where do they live? Why does the size of a flock of sheep depend on your mother's brother? What is *tchindi?*

At least that was the way it worked out for me when I showed it.

I showed it to sixth-grade students; they burst out in questions.

I showed it to their parents; they burst out in questions.

I showed it to my college classes; they burst out in questions.

And all the groups found their own answers in what they had heard. It took a discussion to bring it all out. The whole group, cooperating and remembering various comments from that "young man," found most of the answers. Wrong guesses were corrected by others.

But enough questions were left to prick them on to more learning, more reading, more probing. One value of inquiry is that it leaves you curious and unsatisfied; you want to learn more.

*   *   *

Ted explained. "You give the students information. Try to make it provocative also. Then you ask them to figure out what's going on. You might ask them: 'If these are the answers, what were the questions?' You might even have them list the questions they think are important."

Ted was an anthropologist and archaeologist who had worked on restoring Plimoth Plantation south of Boston and had studied gravestones in New England, tracing the patterns as the stonecutters migrated to different towns. But most importantly for me, he had worked on the Anthropology Curriculum Study Project, an enterprise by professional anthropologists to develop a curriculum for high school students. Ted wrote some of the lessons, he composed some of the problems. He had learned to create lessons of inquiry.

"Inquiry is one name for this approach. Inductive teaching

is another," Bob Spaulding added. "The important thing is to get students to think, not just to memorize. Too darned much of the learning in schools is really rote learning. Instead, we want kids to learn to think, to criticize, to challenge. The only way to do that is to have them practice on thinking, criticizing, and challenging. And that means having teachers who do not talk too much."

Bob Spaulding, a onetime sheepherder, taught education classes at Duke University. Bob knew how to raise provocative questions, how to loop students into the fun of learning.

Now I had the formula from two competent teachers.

The formula for inquiry teaching: Present to the students some interesting and provocative material and ask them what they make of it. Then, when they have it partially worked out, present them with more material, related to the first, supplementary, sometimes contradictory. Keep the kids a bit off balance, because a bit of frustration is needed in order to get us to change our habits of thought, to change our views and prejudices and stereotypes. When we are a little off balance, we do more thinking. If the facts are present, we just might use them in our thinking.

*　　　*　　　*

Now back to what Ray Cloud had taught me up on the reservation. Ray was the old Chippewa who could neither read nor write nor speak English. Yet he learned my kinship chart well enough to catch my error.

One of the lessons for my new curriculum was a chart. It had names on it. Names and dates and circles and triangles and vertical lines and horizontal lines. Figure 1 shows a version of it. Every student studies a copy. Quickly some of the students know what it is. Most do not. The trick is to get those who do know to explain the chart clearly enough to the others. En route, they learn more themselves.

The knowledgeable kids would start right off saying that it was a family tree. So I would ask them to explain the circles.

"Oh, those are girls or women, females. And the triangles are for men."

The follow-up questions are the keys to inquiry teaching.

Figure 1. Kinship Chart.

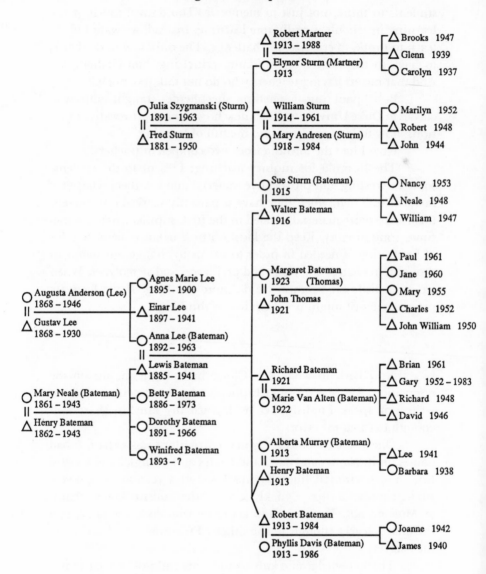

You must remember to use them. Instead of accepting an answer, you ask, "What makes you think that circles represent women?"

"Because the circles are next to names of women."

"Is that true in every part of the chart?"

Pause while they scan. Some of them are uncertain about names such as Einar. Otherwise, they stick with their interpretation.

Again, you don't praise a student for speaking out with the "correct answer." Instead, you ask another student whether he agrees. Then another whether she agrees. In real scientific research, the approval comes from one's peers. You can't peek in the back of the book or just ask the teacher. In real research, the approval comes when the criticism dies down.

Nor do you tell a student that her answer is wrong any more than you would say that her answer is right. Instead, ask another student to make that judgment. "Do you agree?"

There's another reason for encouraging criticism and different opinions. That a student agrees with the teacher does not necessarily mean that the student is right.

An alert class can do wonders with that chart. And any class given the chance to use its brains becomes an alert class.

One of the highest hurdles for the teacher is learning to keep quiet. Just smile. Don't say, "That's right." Don't say, "Good for you." Don't say, "That's wrong." Just smile and ask another student whether he or she agrees. I went in heavily for the amiable grunt and the interested chuckle, both of which sounded noncommittal but had a tone of "That's interesting. Tell us some more."

At first, that lack of approval does frustrate students who know doggone well that their answer was right. They expend their frustration in proving that they were right and convincing others.

When the meaning of circles and triangles and equal signs and horizontal lines and vertical lines is cleared up, then you can ask other questions.

"What would Margaret Bateman call Mary Thomas?"

"What would Margaret call Henry Bateman (1865-1942)?"

"Which names get used often? Which names get dropped? And what happens when a woman gets married? Why?"

"Do you see any patterns of family life here? Patterns in marrying? Patterns in numbers of children? Patterns in life span?"

A next step is to introduce a new chart using the same symbols. In the curriculum we were working on at Airlie House, the chart was of a native group, the people of the first set of slides (see Figure 2). The names were different, the patterns were different, and the rules of naming were different. The class could figure that out quickly. By now, they would also know that the people were Navajo Indians.

Once the joking over the names is done with, you can proceed. I had my students help to make lists of names from our own culture: Henry Clay, Roger Mudd, Carpenter, Butcher, Wright, Smith, Baker, Stillwagon, Sweet, Sauer, Hand, Foote. The giggling stopped. I saved that list and used it with sixth-grade kids, college students, a group of teachers, and a group of parents. They were astonishingly similar in laughing at the names, a common form of ethnocentrism.

"You already know what the symbols mean. The circles and triangles and lines all mean the same as before. Now what can you make of this chart? What questions can you ask of this chart?"

After some initial bewilderment over the repetition of names, which I simply tell them is the Donay system of the Navajo, any class begins to see relationships.

"That Bitter Water woman got married, and all of her kids became Bitter Water. But when Bitter Water men get married, their children follow their mother."

"Is that true in all parts of the chart?"

"And the next generation does, too."

"Do you agree?"

In time, a class can even elicit negative rules. You do not marry certain persons. As they look for patterns, a class will come up with all sorts of ingenious answers that require more data to confirm. You can even distinguish matriarchal from matrilineal, because someone is sure to confuse the two terms.

Usually someone asks what the word *Donay* means. Let the class answer, groping for an English word that covers the relationships discovered.

Elicit is one of the favorite words of teachers who use inquiry methods. They like to elicit understandings out of a chart or an article or a table, to draw them out. When I started using *elicit*

Figure 2. Navajo Donay System.

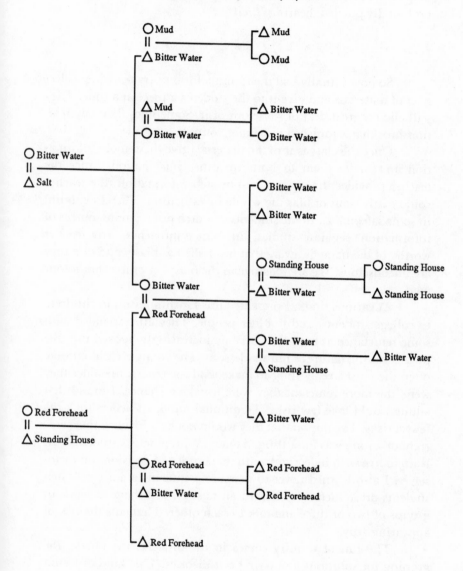

frequently, I found it best to spell it out on a blackboard. Some were profoundly puzzled, hearing *illicit.*

*   *   *

So now I finally had the formula for inquiry teaching: Select a set of materials and give it to the students a piece at a time. They will elicit a great deal of sense out of it. Sometimes they saw relationships that astonished me. Brace yourself.

Once the class is into the material, give them more information and invite them to hunt up other information. Since the teacher provides this sort of step-by-step information, the teacher could easily slant or bias the whole investigation. Therefore, build in some safeguards. Invite students to search out separate sources of information, separate studies, different approaches. Any teacher worthy of the name is aware that he or she has biases and that they are unconscious. We are sensitive to the biases of others, not to our own.

At various times, I presented this kinship lesson to children, to college students, and to older people. They all responded with some reluctance at first, then became increasingly hooked into the puzzle-solving nature of inquiry lessons. The younger children were often the most free, willing to make wild inferences; the older they were, the more reluctant they were to take a chance. I found that adults would take few risks. Traditional-minded teachers took the fewest risks. The notion that they would not be told when they were right or wrong was unsettling to many. With practice, students will learn to live with indecision, with that burden of decisions on themselves. I also learned never to pressure a student to answer. When students are reluctant to hazard an answer, ask them to work in groups of two or three and talk to each other. That cuts the risk of appearing silly.

The fun of inquiry comes in the mystery, the puzzle, the groping for solutions and trying out theories. This kind of lesson seems to have intrinsic interest. Students like it for itself. They seldom worry about grades, once they feel some assurance that their tentative answers will be considered without ridicule. This takes practice for both students and teacher.

On his first glimpse of the family tree, one boy read off "Ole Lee, 1860-1932. That looks like a tombstone." The class laughed. He flushed in embarrassment. Then a class leader agreed with him. "It really is like a tombstone." Slowly, others agreed, and I could see the first boy gaining confidence. Soon all of them were calling an entry "a tombstone," but only if it had both dates.

*   *   *

One reader asked me how I would use inquiry methods to teach what she had studied. Her field was bookkeeping. I don't know. Years ago, I was smart enough to marry a woman who balances our checkbook and keeps the accounts and calculates the taxes. Perhaps some fields of learning are not amenable to inquiry methods; but I doubt it.

One way might be the approach used with the family tree. Present some simple pages from an account book along with the invoices and bills and income and let students figure out the conventions for entries, the rules for using them. Let them reason out why. Don't tell them; let them think. Later, give them some pages with errors. But don't tell them that errors exist. Let them find out. More advanced classes could be given doctored books and asked to find the shenanigans slipped in there by the embezzler. Or find out whether any had been slipped in.

I don't know how to apply the method to other fields. When I began teaching, I determined to learn a lot about what I was teaching. That meant that I had less time for other things. So I remain firmly and determinedly ignorant of enormous fields of knowledge: music, internal combustion engines, games played with balls, the philosophy of Swedenborg, computer language, modern genetics beyond the Punnet Square, and bookkeeping. The list is much, much longer, but I don't wish to boast.

Some smart teacher who does know bookkeeping will figure it out.

*   *   *

Now that I had the formula, I began creating my own lessons of inquiry. Some were pretty good.

Some were dreadful.

They were too difficult or too simple or too dull. But often such lessons can be salvaged by restructuring and rewriting, just as my slide show on the desert was salvaged. The chapters that follow contain many examples of this. If you are a teacher, feel free to use them. If you are a parent, feel free to encourage their use by the teachers of your offspring, those with the big brains. In either case, feel free to treat them as puzzles to enjoy. Feel free to borrow, adopt, adapt, revise, change, or shamelessly swipe. However, you may not sell them.

*   *   *

The first problem for the student in deciphering the kinship chart was to discover the rules for making a chart. The discovery is aimed at the conventions. What does this symbol mean? Does it always mean that?

One way to determine understanding is to violate the rules and see whether others catch it. For example:

"I have here a bronze coin with the head of Julius Caesar and the date of 43 B.C. on the reverse. That's the year after he was stabbed to death. It is badly corroded and looks quite old. How much do you think it's worth?"

I sketch two circles on the board, then draw a head in one and "43 B.C." in the other.

"Ten dollars."

"Twenty."

"It's a fake."

The class turns and stares at the iconoclast. He grins with self-assurance. "The date of 43 B.C. could not have been written till A.D. They didn't use that system of numbering years then. They couldn't have. They didn't know it was forty-three years ahead of something that hadn't happened yet."

Most of the class will laugh and agree. But some will look puzzled.

Quickly, someone else repeats the explanation in different

words. Light dawns. Nobody knew about the birth of Christ until after it. And the system of numbering years from that date actually started five centuries later. Dates with B.C. in them appear only in history books, retrospectively. The ancients did not count backward.

A hesitant hand comes up. "I think that there's something else wrong with the coin. You've got the date in our type of number, but the Romans didn't use that kind. They used *X*'s and *V*'s and *I*'s. So whoever made that counterfeit used the wrong system of numbering."

"How should it be written?"

"Four *X*'s and three *I*'s."

I write on the board: XXXXIII.

"Well, maybe it should be *X* something *III*. What is the letter used for fifty? It really is fifty, minus ten, plus three,"

"Who knows?" The answer comes that *L* stood for fifty.

I write her number on the board: XLIII. There is some nodding of heads. And some bewilderment among those who learned Roman numerals in the fourth grade and promptly forgot them. Quickly we review the system.

1	I				
2	II				
3	III				
4	IV or IIII				
5	V	50	L	500	D
6	VI				
7	VII				
8	VIII				
9	IX	90	XC	900	CM
10	X	100	C	1000	M
15	XV	115	CXV	1015	MXV

Stressing the subtractive position is important. If an *I* is in front of a higher number, you subtract. If the *I* is after it, you add. Thus, IV equals our four, but VI equals our six. Using the same principle, we get XL for forty and XC for ninety and MCM for 1900.

"Now I want each of you to write 1987 in Roman numerals. Help each other. Work together." Heads bow together around the room as they cooperate. They struggle with 1987 in Roman numerals and at last come up with MCMLXXXVII. The faster ones explain it to the laggards.

In my classes, students help each other a lot, and there is a lot of leaning over and writing on other students' notes. Except during tests.

"Where would you see such a date?"

"On cornerstones."

"On movies. They put the date in Roman numerals, but you have to read fast to see it."

"That's because they don't want you to know how old that movie is."

"Now I have a cornerstone with the date on it. Here is the date: I IX VIII VII."

Staring, followed by dawning understanding, followed by giggles.

"Whoever did that didn't know his numerals. He just changed the individual numbers of 1987 into Roman numbers. But the Romans would never have done it that way."

"They didn't use spaces like that, and they didn't know anything about position value. No way could they have used that first capital *I* to mean one thousand."

At this point occurred one of those leaps of understanding that delight a teacher but leave most of the class dismayed and blank. A girl spoke up. "Let's see you write the date 1980 using that system."

I laughed and wrote I IX VIII and then paused. She looked at me triumphantly. I wrote a zero. She laughed. A few of the class joined her, but only a few.

Back to the basics to explain. The Romans had no zero. The zero came with the Arabic system, which we use today. And that is based on position value. Zero is the sign for an empty position. For some of this, you must give brief lectures.

In 1987, the 7 means just a simple 7 in Arabic.

The 8 means 8 times 10 or 80.

The 9 means 9 times a hundred, or 900.

The 1 means 1 times a thousand, which makes 1,000.

Add them up and you get one thousand nine hundred and eighty-seven.

At the blackboard, I circled the I IX VIII VII and labeled it "counterfeit." The same for the one with the fake zero. The Roman coin with 43 B.C. is also labeled counterfeit.

*   *   *

Now, there was a point to all this number business, and I soon came to it with the tale of the Kensington Stone, found on a farm in Minnesota in 1898 with ancient Scandinavian runic writing carved on it. The runes were deciphered to read like this:

> 8 Goths and 22 Norwegians on exploration journey from Vinland over the West. We had camp by 2 sker-ries one days journey north from this stone. We were and fished one day. After we came home 10 red with blood and dead Ave Maria Save from evil
>   Have 10 of our party by the sea to look after our ships 14 days journey from this island Year 1362

A quick lesson in runic numbers.

The whole system was much like this (it varied over the centuries and in different parts of Scandinavian influence; see Wahlgren, 1958):

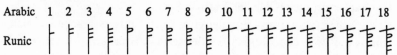

| Arabic | 1 | 2 | 3 | 4 | 5 | 6 | 7 | 8 | 9 | 10 | 11 | 12 | 13 | 14 | 15 | 16 | 17 | 18 |

Now there is a real lesson in inquiry. What are the rules? A class will figure that out fast.

You can explain that runic numbers did not go very high. If the number was large, they spelled it out.

Now, pay attention to this:

For 22, the Kensington stone had:

For 14, it had:

The class studied those and began to giggle.

For the year 1362, the Kensington Stone had: .

The folks who first translated the runes said that that was the date 1362. Runic experts from Scandinavia laughed, just as my class did.

"Why, that's a fraud. It's the same dumb mistake that was made with the Roman numerals."

"The guy who wrote that mixed up two systems, the runes and the Arabic system."

As before, we spell out the problem. The runic "one," which was written ⌐ , has suddenly developed the value of one thousand, as if it were an Arabic place number. The runic "three" (⌐) has suddenly gained the value of three hundred.

If you can believe that a lost Viking crew with one-third of their men killed by the natives would stick around long enough to cut a stone block and then chisel a message, you probably can also believe that the same Vikings, under great pressure, would absent-mindedly invent the decimal system, thus leaving a message that no other Viking could read.

When it comes to counterfeiting, it is the little things that trip you up.

Or the systems of thought so ingrained in us that we don't realize them consciously—such big things can also trip you up. Our systems of thought are ingrained in our language, as mentioned in the chapter on race (Chapter Eight).

Notice that I am not denying that Vikings reached North America. The archaeological evidence at L'Anse-aux-Meadows in Newfoundland is solid and clear. This analysis argues that one alleged piece of evidence in Minnesota is a fake.

*   *   *

So maybe the Vikings did not bring civilization to the poor Indians. Maybe it was the Egyptians or the Irish or the Jews or the Chinese.

That set of speculations deserves its own chapter.

11

Checking the Evidence: Pyramids and Chariots

One by-product of race prejudice is fake history. If we assume that the American Indians were inferior in intelligence, it is easy to believe that any cultural advance they had was not really produced by Indians but by some lost Irishman or lost Viking or lost Egyptian or lost Israelite or lost Greek. Maybe even by some bug-eyed monster from outer space.

I'm not making this up. Ever since Columbus returned to Spain, writers have speculated about the Indians and who they were and where they came from. The speculations have included lost Irishmen, lost Vikings, lost Egyptians, lost Israelites, and lost Greeks. Only recently have some of our loonies credited the space aliens.

The proof is obvious. The Aztecs built pyramids. The Egyptians built pyramids. Therefore, someone, somehow sailed over from Egypt and taught the dumb Aztecs how to build pyramids. How else could they get pyramids? Nobody speculated that maybe the Aztecs sailed over to teach the dumb Egyptians how to build pyramids.

My purpose as a teacher was threefold. I wanted to establish the evidence for the Indians as perfectly competent members of the human race. I wanted the students to learn something about the Neolithic period, which covers the domestication of animals and plants and the invention of pottery. And I wanted them to learn how to handle evidence in testing a theory. Those are three big goals.

So I posed this question: *Was the development of the Neolithic in the Americas linked to the development of the Neolithic in the Near East?* In other words: Are the American Indian civilizations of the Mayas and the Aztecs and the Incas a local product, locally invented, or were they diffused from the Old World centers of Egypt and Sumeria? Since this involves our major foods, both plants and animals, we have much to compare.

It isn't easy. Most people have very little knowledge of where our food came from or how it was first grown.

Let's begin with some major plants first grown in gardens and farms in the Near East and in the Americas. Here are two lists:

Region A	*Region B*
maize (corn)	wheat
kidney beans	barley
lima beans	rye
jack beans	rice
scarlet runner	apples
avocado	oranges
squash	figs
potatoes	dates
cacao (chocolate)	olives
tomatoes	root crops (beets, car-
peanuts	rots, and so on)
pineapple	
tobacco	
coca	
quinine	

Common to Both

coconut
sweet potatoes

Can you tell where each region is?

Some people challenge the accuracy of the list. Many insist that potatoes came from Ireland, that chocolate comes from Switzerland, that coca and chocolate are the same thing. Nowadays they more readily identify coca with cocaine.

But they usually accept that Region A is the Americas and Region B is the Near East and related areas.

Establishing the locale is also a way to make them familiar with the lists. One good source is Charles B. Heiser, Jr.'s (1973) *From Seed to Civilization*. That may settle most arguments. A very recent book probably has a wider scope than food plants. Jack Weatherford (1988) wrote an account of all the foods and skills and products that American Indians devised or domesticated. The title of his book is *Indian Givers: How the Indians of the Americas Transformed the World*.

Then the class gets another pair of lists:

sheep	guinea pig
goat	llama
pig	alpaca
cattle	turkey
horse	
ass	
elephant	

Common to Both

dog

This one is easier. They know the game now and quickly assign the first list of domesticated animals to the Old World and the short second list to the Americas. Usually someone argues about the horses, "Indians had horses, didn't they?" If you are lucky, some student knows that the horses used by the Indians descended from those that escaped from Coronado in 1540. Having a student who knows some history makes it easier for the rest of them to accept. For in this type of teaching, the teacher tries to avoid sounding like the voice of authority. If they seem dubious, send them to the library.

So? What do the lists mean?

The Neolithic developments seemed to be separate. Even the most avid defender of diffusion across the Atlantic has a hard time making much out of those utterly different lists of garden crops and domesticated animals other than "no contact." But a few will make a stab at it.

"Couldn't they have brought over the *idea* of planting seeds and then used local seeds?"

Let the class answer. If they were colonizing farmers, what would they bring? If the contacts were a few shipwrecked sailors, what would most likely happen?

*   *   *

"What kind of evidence do you need in addition to just these lists?"

"How about other similarities? Artwork? Numbers? Writing? Temples? Religious beliefs? Pottery? Pyramids? Language? Weapons?"

Hesitantly, some of them come up with speculations. Perhaps the archaeological record would reveal a sequence of development or a sudden new intrusion. A thought as abstract as that baffles some and intrigues others until we translate it into the specific example of various Indian sites in Minnesota with stone tools in the lower levels and then the intrusion of trade goods in the upper, more recent levels. When you read the kind of chart that lists the items found at such sites, you are going back in time as you go down in the strata. The top is recent.

1. Steel knives, steel axes, iron kettles, glass beads, glass bottles, bullets, guns, cloth
2. Pottery bowls with handles, stone points, stone knives, ground stone axes, copper fish hooks, bone hoes
3. Crude pottery, stone points, bone points, flaked points, some copper tools (native copper)
4. Copper knife, grooved stone ax, stone gouge, copper awl, chipped stone points and knives
5. Beautifully flaked stone points, some fluted, shell pendant

Now since we know the history of the invasion of whites into North America with iron, steel, glass, and blankets, we know that those items were not invented by the Chippewa or the Sioux. They were trade goods. They appear suddenly in the strata of a dig, and the presence of glass beads tells the digger what year that level was. He or she cross-checks with written history.

Then the class gets some assigned readings. They get Robert Braidwood's studies in Iraqi Kurdistan at a site called Jarmo, where successive levels of a Neolithic village show the growth of techniques in growing and storing wheat and in developing a new strain of wheat. They also show the slow development of domesticated sheep and goats as shown by the increasing number of bones.

They also get a reading by Richard MacNeish on the valley of Tehuacan in Mexico, where his crew dug up successive layers revealing the gradual domestication of squash and beans and maize. The early cobs of corn (maize) were about the size of a little finger. The time spans several thousand years.

And then they get material on the pyramids. They read I.E.S. Edwards' (1947) book on *The Pyramids of Egypt*, showing the gradual development from underground tombs with simple mastabas over them to the first stepped pyramid at Sakkara, made of small stones, to the larger ones at Giza, made of large stones.

And they generalize about the Egyptian pyramids to answer questions about the purpose, the method of construction, the design, the history of changes in design, and the materials of construction.

1. All of them were designed as tombs.
2. All of them were made of carefully cut and shaped stones.
3. All of the Egyptian pyramids also had a temple complex at the side, usually toward the Nile.

And then they learn of the slow development of the pyramidal style in Mexico, beginning with the oldest at Cuicuilco, which was circular, with steps leading up to each flat and terraced level. For this, I usually lectured using my own notes from the University of Mexico and my own slides. Then they generalize about Mexican pyramids.

1. All of them were flat on top as a platform for temples.
2. None were tombs for burial (with one or two exceptions).
3. Their construction was of stone, but only the exterior was of shaped stone. The interior was rubble.
4. All of them had staircases on the western side leading to the temple on the flat top of the terraced pyramid.
5. Many of them were enlarged every fifty-two years, with the new built right over the old.

And we learn of the construction methods. In Egypt, the great stones were carefully measured and cut. In Mexico, only the surface stones were cut; inside, the workmen dumped uncut and unshaped stones, apparently carrying baskets of rock and gravel as fill.

So how stands the argument for contact and diffusion against the argument for independent invention?

Since this makes a pretty convincing display, it is time for some contrary evidence. Ask several students to look up pictures and descriptions of the temples in Sumeria, which were often placed on top of terraced pyramids, the ziggurats, also called the Hanging Gardens.

The new puzzle of looking for similarities and diffusion will lead to some sharp class discussions. Remember that the goal is learning how to test ideas against data rather than memorizing the data. How could students keep from learning interesting stuff like that?

The goal is helping students to develop the skills to grow on their own time.

*   *   *

Much more can be used in such a lesson. The systems of writing in the Near East are reasonably well known: cuneiform in Sumeria, hieroglyphs in Egypt, alphabets in Phoenicia and Greece. Where do you get samples of such writing to show to a class? From encyclopedias and histories in the library. I used a Dover edition of the *Book of the Dead* for Egyptian hieroglyphics and also a Dover edition of a Mayan codex for pictographic writing in colored pictures. Put samples in front of the class and let them decide whether they can detect any influence to or from America. To or from America. That usually shakes them up.

More fun was comparing the number systems with all those in the Mediterranean area, based on ten (a decimal system), with the Aztec system, based on twenty (a vigesimal system). The calendars and the religious cycles spark interest in students, and many of them will begin studying on their own if only you shove them in the right direction. Numbers? Look in the *Encyclopaedia Britannica* and copy down examples of one to twenty in Egyptian, in cuneiform, in Greek, in Roman, in Runic. They are all based on ten, and the cuneiform is also based on sixty, which is why we have sixty minutes in an hour.

Then when you hit those students with a picture of a Mayan calendar stela with the base of twenty and a concept for zero and a system of glyphs and dots and bars, most of them will doubt the diffusionists. They will begin to remember the slow development as shown in the archaeological record told by MacNeish and Braidwood, and they will begin to accept the competence of the American Indians.

But not all believe. And that is okay, too. Your job is not to persuade students to a particular conclusion but to teach them how to test a theory against facts and how to gather some facts. As a parent, you would not want teachers to indoctrinate even that which you believe to be true. A logical conclusion can be revised; indoctrination, given as revealed and absolute, is a hard pattern to remake.

This is as good a place as any to mention that tired old misused quotation, "The exception proves the rule." The word *proves* in that sentence does not mean to justify or clinch with argument. It means to test. Our military tests new cannon or new tanks on the "proving ground." An exception tests the rule. If you find an exception, you had better modify your rule. Evidence against your rule does not mean that your rule is correct; it means just the opposite.

We borrowed the phrase from Latin: *Exceptio probat regulam,* meaning "An exception tests the rule." Just think of how

many times someone faced with evidence against his or her pet
theory has shouted out that contrary evidence actually supports it.

But don't expect to dislodge the fanatics who believe that
beings from outer space came to earth to teach the Indians how to
build pyramids and to grow corn. The only thing that might budge
their minds is detailed knowledge of the local developmental history of buildings and of the archaeological record of crops such as
MacNeish found. True believers seldom study such technical stuff.

*   *   *

One more set of lists:

Transport

dugouts	plank ships
birchbark canoes	sails
small reed rafts	large reed boats
skin boats	skin boats
paddles	oars in banks
dog with travois	wheel (cart, wagon, chariot)
llama	horse, ox

One item in that list is crucial. Which single item would not
be forgotten by sailor or farmer or explorer who was cast upon an
alien shore and then attempted to enlighten the natives?

The Indians of North and South America never used the
wheel. Only one example of the wheel has been found, one crude
little toy in Mexico made of pottery.

Much more can be done with such a comparison of the Neolithic developments and then Bronze Age developments. Using the
tension of questioning a myth and having the students debunk it
leads to long-term learning.

Encourage students to bring in data. Bring in articles or pictures or evidence that contradict or support any view in class.

*   *   *

Once a student skilfully argued that a single stranger wandering by himself could seriously influence the natives. He used the survival of Cabeza de Vaca in the southern areas of what is now the United States as evidence that lost sailors could survive in a hostile environment.

He was encouraged to read the account of the Spaniards under Narváez who landed in 1527 in Florida and, after losing their ships, struggled barefoot and naked across Texas, New Mexico, Arizona, and finally back to Mexico City. Only four men survived the bitter eight-year struggle. And they did leave some influence. They converted many of the tribes to Christianity and engaged in what we would call faith healing.

But, the student told the class, any conversion was soon undone by the actions of the other Spaniards who came in with horses, armor, and muskets to kill or enslave many of those same Indians who had just been converted.

This is a provocative series of lessons.

But the stress should lie on solving a problem. How do you determine whether a theory is supported?

All parts of this lesson lead easily into writing essays in which the student must take a position and organize many facts to support that position.

Exam questions can easily be constructed around comparing the development of the Neolithic in two distinct regions. The food plants, the domesticated animals, the methods of agriculture, the use of the Nile floodings, the terraces of the Peruvian Andes, or the cold weather strategies of the ancient farmers around Lake Titicaca—all of these suggest opportunities for students to show off their knowledge and display their writing skills. Or you can construct questions modeled after the suggestions in Ben Bloom's taxonomy described in Chapter Nine.

My favorite was the basic issue of diffusion versus independent invention, and some form of it usually appeared as one option in the exam questions. My classes studied several exam questions in advance, with the actual selection coming as a surprise on exam day. This sort of warning focused review quite sharply and led to long-term retention. Students had time to compare notes, organize answers, argue with each other, and learn which bits of knowledge must be learned or which could be stored on a cheat card.

A cheat card was one three-by-five card with notes of all the stuff a student could not remember. They could cram notes onto it in tiny writing and lay the card openly on their desks.

Guess what happens when you write down what you find hard to remember? An hour later you discover that you have learned everything on your card. So you write another one. The cheat card was a superb tool for review.

*   *   *

Implicit in most of these arguments is the law of parsimony, sometimes called Occam's razor. When you are groping for an explanation, the rule is to accept the theory that makes the fewest assumptions.

Occam's razor sounds magnificent in Latin: *Entia non sunt multiplicanda praeter necessitatem*—"Entities are not to be multiplied beyond necessity." That's what I used to say about Occam until Bertrand Russell corrected me. Russell was dead at the time; I read it in his *A History of Western Philosophy* (Russell, 1967). He said that the great Latin sentence was never actually found in Occam, but what Occam wrote comes out even finer in English: "It is vain to do with more what can be done with fewer."

Or put into very simple detective-story English: "Don't blame the murder on the Martians when the trail of blood leads to the butler's pantry."

12

Discovering
Insights:
Pumpkin Pie

School laboratories can be great places for discovery. They are also great places for gaining insight.

When Gordon Meyers reaches the lessons on blood in his class in anatomy and physiology, he notices that student interest picks up. They are getting ready to sample their own blood in order to analyze it for those white blood cells which reveal infections.

First they learn some skills: How do you count white blood cells on a slide? Meyers, who teaches at the same community college in Rochester where I taught, makes some slides of his own blood, stains them, and makes a differential white blood cell count several times to get a range from a high count to a low count.

Then the students make the count on the teacher's blood until they can consistently get within that range. Counting blood cells through a microscope takes skill; skill takes practice.

Then Meyers cuts their fingers to smear their own blood on the glass. To save class time, he also stains and prepares all the slides. Then they count. They have five different types of white cells to count, and they want to know the percentage of each. They ignore the red cells.

How do you determine percentages? Either you can divide your count by the total, or you can keep track of your count until you reach a total of 100. Then the count of 5 out of 100 is the same as 5 percent. They do it the easy way.

The students check their count against the normal percentages. Am I normal? That is an important question.

Suddenly the textbook begins to come alive. That's my blood there, and a high count could mean that I have an infection. The white blood cells increase to counter infection.

The illustrations in the text suddenly seem real. The pictures actually look like real blood cells.

Insight comes in many ways. But it usually means that you gain a deeper and richer understanding of a concept that you have already learned. Now it is not just words to memorize; it is real.

And the safety precautions routinely warned about become far more meaningful when your own finger has a cut in it and so does everyone else's finger and you remember the warning about AIDS and about hepatitis and how easy it is to touch someone else's blood or to nick yourself on a tiny razor.

Learning in books needs frequent reference to life.

*   *   *

I observed a similar intensity of purpose and rising of interest in a class on microbiology taught by Jerry Tammen. Microbes and bacteria seem to inhabit only textbooks and prepared slides until one day when each student brings in a sample of water. Students who live in the country are urged to bring a jar from their own water faucet from their home well. The city students, whose city water is filtered and chlorinated, can get their samples from ponds and rivers and other possibly contaminated places.

What do they do with their samples? Some of them first test for nitrates, which could most likely come from fertilizer spread on the fields that has leached into the groundwater and thus contaminated a well. They pour a bit of their sample into one of two glass tubes held in a box and add a bit of a reagent that attaches to any nitrate present and colors the water. The more nitrate, the darker the yellow. The other tube holds clear water. You can see the difference in color; the water with nitrates is yellow.

The box has a rotating set of filters of increasing yellowness.

You match the colors, then read the nitrate amount directly from the filter. Very quick and very simple. While I watched, one student got a zero rating. Clean. No nitrates. The next one got a reading of ten, the highest possible. She told me that her water came from a farm pond and was sure to be contaminated. She was delighted to have such a high score, because it confirmed her prediction.

The second test is for coliform bacteria, which are the ones that grow in feces and could get into well water from a leaky septic tank or, more likely, from a feedlot with lots of cattle. The procedure is to make three tests of the water, reducing the amount of water in each sample to one-tenth the size of the previous sample. First they pour 10 milliliters into a test tube, then 1 milliliter into a second, and then 0.1 milliliter into the last. Each sample is poured through a paper filter to collect the bacteria. Then each filter is labeled and placed carefully in a small culture dish with some nutrient to feed the bacteria.

The covered dishes are put into an incubator. The bacteria grow and multiply and grow and multiply. In twenty-four hours, the green colonies of fecal bacteria have grown large enough to be visible to the naked eye, each colony growing from one tiny coliform bacterium. Now the students begin to discover the purpose of testing three samples. Sometimes the smallest sample has nothing visible, but a count can yet be taken on the others. The filter is helpfully printed with a grid to make counting easier. And sometimes the concentrated sample is entirely covered with green coliform, making it impossible to count. Usually, you can get two counts out of three for an average.

Suddenly the warnings of the environmentalists that groundwaters are being contaminated by excessive fertilizer and by uncontrolled feedlots choked with manure begin to take on real meaning. It happens right here. That becomes a fertile insight.

It is a shocking experience to discover that you have been drinking out of a toilet.

Jerry Tammen told me that rarely did a student fail to get personally involved in this experiment. The one who forgot his sample seemed serenely untroubled. "He's flunking his tests, so I doubt that he will last many weeks longer." Jerry shrugged.

I found myself hoping that he would flunk out. I really

would not want that guy in charge of testing any water that I might drink.

Discoveries and insights flourish in laboratories because you must apply what you have learned to living things. In that application, you strengthen your knowledge of all the related concepts. They become translated from mere words into real insights, clearer understandings.

*   *   *

Laboratories need not be indoors. A geologist prefers to hike his students to a cutbank where all can see the strata laid down over millions of years.

Ron Hall does more than just show his students a cutbank when he teaches geology. First he gives them a geological map of the county, then he takes them to a site and asks them to locate the place on the map. That is an interesting puzzle. You must be able to read the map well enough to see what it means, and you must be able to read the strata well enough to see what the connection is to the map.

"Scale throws them at first," said Ron. "If one kind of rock is twenty feet thick, that looks enormous at the cutbank. But on the map, it's pretty tiny."

So you learn. You compare with your fellow students. You hike up and down, and you measure the strata, and you argue some more with your classmates. Hall has learned to let the students do the thinking and not be cut off by the first person who guesses the right answer. That person must prove it to the rest of them. As with most real learning, the right answer is not nearly as important as knowing how you got that answer. Those who know how they reached an answer can readily persuade others.

*   *   *

Laboratories can be anywhere. Discoveries and insights come to those who are already tuned to recognize them when they appear.

"I waited to be last in the elevator. Then I stood inside the doors facing the other passengers. I grabbed some eye contact and began talking with them. Just casual stuff. Weather. Baseball."

"How did they react?"

"They were paralyzed. Some kept their heads down. Nobody would talk. Nobody would even agree that the sun was shining outside. When the elevator stopped, several scuttled out; I had a suspicion that some of them got off too early just to escape me. I was smiling and polite all the time. At least I thought so. I was neatly dressed and clean. They seemed to think I was nuts."

"And what is the norm?"

"Well, I guess that in elevators, you are expected to face the front, avoid eye contact, and not talk to strangers. I tried the same approach in a line at the post office, and nobody minded. They just picked up a casual and friendly conversation. It might be something about the closed-in space of the elevator."

Most of our lives are regular and predictable because we do what others expect of us and they do what we expect of them. All of our daily living is governed by norms, the term sociologists use for all those customs that are so second nature that we don't ever think of them. Try telling a group of high school or college kids that they are almost totally regulated by custom, and they will laugh. They do their own thing. They're independent, free-willed, freethinking. Nobody tells them what to do.

How can a teacher break through that crust? How can you help them gain insight? How can you help them to see that their behavior is ruled by forces outside themselves, by the combined expectations of others? You give the class an assignment.

"One way you can learn what norms are like is to observe people's behavior, learn their norms, and then violate a norm. Don't pick a major rule, just a little, minor, itty-bitty one that won't hurt. Notice how other people respond. That's an assignment for tomorrow. Violate one minor norm and tell us what happened."

That was why that student faced the crowd in the elevator.

Another student misbuttoned his shirt with one side up and the other down. Whenever someone helpfully pointed this out to him, he thanked them. "Then I just buttoned it wrong in the other direction as I was walking away from them. Soon someone else would tell me, and I would do it again, one button off each time. In the first hour at school, eight of my friends and three teachers told me. I guess most of them didn't want to see me make a fool of myself."

One stylish young woman deliberately clashed her color combinations. Her friends noticed and asked whether she was feeling all right.

Another student regularly helped her mother set the supper table.

"Last night I brought out the best silver from the buffet. Mom threw a fit. She saved that for best. No use to waste good stuff on just family.

"So I put the silver away and used the kitchen stuff, but I put out only a knife and a fork. No spoons. We never use spoons, except for cereal at breakfast. Mom threw another fit, saying that I should know how to set a table now that I was nineteen years old.

"When I cleared the table, all five spoons were just sitting there. Mom put them back in the drawer."

One young woman worked as a waitress in a coffee shop in the largest hotel in town.

"I was wondering what norms I could break when I picked up two orders for pumpkin pie. Suddenly it came to me. I carried them over to the customers and carefully placed them down with the points facing away from the customers.

"Then I set down clean forks and smiled and asked whether they wanted more coffee.

They didn't say a thing. They looked at the pie and they looked up at me and they looked down at the pie again. Then they carefully turned the pies around and started eating. As I walked away, I could hear them whispering. I brought more coffee anyway.

"Three more times that night I did the same thing. I sure picked up a lot of stares.

"The final time, my boss saw me do it and bawled me out. He told me that I should know the right way to serve pie. And I got only tiny tips from those people, too."

Thus a student learns. She becomes aware of the multiplicity of tiny rules that govern our lives and rule our expectations of others and their expectations of us. Many of these students kept on testing norms. Throughout the quarter, they would tell about minor norms that they kept on discovering: ways of eating, of dressing, of greeting, of walking, of waving, of talking, of standing, of sitting, of touching. Somehow, they always giggled when they reported a newly discovered norm.

The original assignment carried some warnings. Don't violate any major rule. Don't violate a rule in such a way that others will get excited or fearful. And don't violate laws.

* * *

A few students always sneered at the experience. They were above such silly stuff. I warned them that if they couldn't come up with a norm to break, I would assign them one. I did.

The first student I selected was a studiedly casual chap. He wasn't slovenly, but close to it. All his clothes were ragged but clean. He slouched a lot. His language was a bit risque, but not really foul-mouthed. He was a middle-class kid going to college and playing out a cool role that hundreds of his friends were also playing. But he didn't realize it. He wore his crowd's uniform, spoke his crowd's language, and felt comfortably inconspicuous.

In the privacy of my office, I told him what I wanted him to do. First I challenged him.

"Now this particular little project requires some nerve. Most of those students probably couldn't cope with it. I think you can."

"Of course I can. What is it?"

"Well, this one involves violating the norms of some of your friends."

"I can do that easy enough."

"Good, I was sure you had guts enough. Here's the plan. Tomorrow you come to school dressed up in your best suit. White shirt. Tie. Shoes shined. As if you were going to a church wedding with a formal party afterward."

"Oh, no." His face was stricken.

"All your friends will make comments. And I want you to write down those comments, but never in front of anyone. And don't tell anyone that you are doing an experiment. Don't give the game away."

After a struggle, he finally agreed. He did not know it, but we had switched from violating a norm to overdoing the norm, in effect violating the norm at the upper end of the curve.

Next day when I saw him in the hallway in his neat clothes, he grinned self-consciously, so different from his buddies. In class several hours later, he reported from his notes: "That was the craziest experience I ever had. I live in a rooming house nearby, and when I came down all dressed up, my landlady just yelled at me. 'You're crazy to dress up like that just to go to that crummy college.' "

He read on from his notes. "I walked in the west door, and Mr. Jansen saw me and asked me to teach his class and then laughed."

"Then Jim here," he pointed to another student, "says to me, 'Are you getting married?' And Alice said the same thing, and Lorna and Tom and Peter all asked me if I was getting married. They were really piling on the peer pressure to make me conform. Then Peter saw me again and yelled, 'Are you getting married or buried?' And then he led the razzing. By that time, I was beginning to enjoy the whole show. I had never realized how much pressure to conform there really is. I had to duck into the can to write my notes. All my friends keep bragging how independent they are and how nobody can tell them how to do anything. But they were the guys who were forcing me to conform. And they all dress alike and talk alike and think alike."

Peter objected loudly. The class hooted. The class was gaining insight into norms and conformity and peer pressure.

The waitress with the pumpkin pie laughed aloud. "You don't have to be a boss to make people conform. I think that most of the pressure on me comes from my friends."

Heads nodded around the room. They were gaining insight into a system of social control. The girl who clashed colors grinned agreement.

Insight is precious. It happens when we suddenly see relationships, when we suddenly understand, when we grasp the meaning of a complex problem because we see it being acted out in front of us.

The "dressing up in your best suit" experience was one that could be used by a teacher year after year. It was.

Not always did the student gain insight. Some just got angry, often at me.

Usually, someone would notice that the norm of behavior in dressing was to pressure the person not to dress up. There seemed to be upper and lower limits of normative behavior that we tolerate.

You cannot be too sloppy or too elegant. Once a class could grasp that one, they also could grasp the pressure not to get the highest grade in class or, at least, the pressure not to let others know that you got the highest. Or the pressure to boast about how much you had to drink or how fast you drove a car or how many laws you had broken.

Perhaps the least gain in insight came to an unfortunate boy who was assigned to review his driver training manual and to drive for one day with scrupulous regard for the laws. He was to stay under the speed limit. He was to yield the right of way to every pedestrian. He was to make a full stop at each stop sign. And he was to be courteous to other drivers, yielding graciously.

He told the class what happened.

"I had to drive my dad to work, and he was late. I kept the speed under thirty, and he got mad. Then I stopped to wave a pedestrian across, and my dad blew his stack. I made a full stop at the stop sign, and he told me that if I couldn't drive any better than that, I couldn't have the car any more."

The student went on. "This is about the dumbest thing I've ever done for a class. It didn't do any good. I didn't learn anything. All it did was to make my father mad at me."

But the rest of the class, after they had stopped laughing, discussed the pressure to obey norms, even those that are illegal. Several told of how they had been assigned, as youngsters, to keep watch for the cops out the rear window and to warn dad to slow down. As he listened to other stories, the angry young driver slowly seemed to gain a bit of insight, a little bit.

When students begin to understand what some parents are doing to them, the teacher might be in trouble. A teacher who alerts his or her students to the way in which their parents violate laws can easily be labeled subversive. It is a risk of the occupation, as some king once said about assassinations.

Insights come in many ways, often accidentally. But the student's mind must be prepared with an underlying concept before the insight can occur. First you learn the meaning, and then you say, "Aha, now I see how it works." This is a bit like learning a new word and then noticing how often you hear it.

Gaining insight takes a huge step forward in challenging the assumptions of our daily life. And challenging assumptions leads to critical thinking.

*   *   *

Social scientists use the term *probability* quite often. My colleague Bill Walton, who taught creative problem solving in a class that the catalogue labeled "Physics," once worked out an improvement on the familiar student science fair project designed to display a normal frequency curve.

For years, high school kids have made a series of vertical columns of plexiglass. You dumped a bucket of marbles in the top; they bounced against pegs to create some scatter and then fell into one of the columns. Most of them fell in the center column, fewer in those nearby, and fewest in the far-out columns. The slope of the marbles at the top of each column forms a normal frequency curve, a bell-shaped curve, the commonest picture of probability.

But Bill realized the drawback. "When a kid dumps a bucket of marbles, they all bounce and stack up in the columns. But it happens too fast for them to learn."

Instead, Bill provided only one marble. He also had a grid paper on which he had drawn vertical columns. Each time he dropped the marble, he blacked in a square on the corresponding column. He could see the random nature of the bouncing. Yet one by one, the black spots, first here, then there, piled up into a bell-shaped curve. A large cumulation of random shots filled out the normal frequency curve.

"Now kids will spend an hour or two trying to defeat the normal frequency curve. They are gaining insight into probability."

"Do they ever defeat it? Do they ever come up with a lopsided curve?"

"With a few tries, yes. Not yet with a hundred trials. It's fun to watch some kid getting excited when he has his first three drops fall way off on the right. By the time he's dropped a marble ten times, the curve is leveling off. By fifty, it's close to bell-shaped, and by a hundred it's the usual normal frequency curve. Theoretically, it could happen; it's not likely to. I should say improbable."

Well, I didn't have the mechanics to do that in my classes.

But I could pull a half dollar out of my pocket and flip it, announce the result as heads, and then ask what the next flip would get. Most students would confidently say tails, the opposite of the first toss. Only a few would make each flip independent of the last. Careful recording leads them to insight.

And that careful observation comes only by long lists of predictions matched against actual results for a flip. It works. When they flip a coin a hundred times, recording each prediction next to the result and then totaling their scores, they begin to understand simple probabilities. Adding up the scores for the whole class gives a new insight: Each flip is independent. The coin has no memory.

That insight comes variously for different students, some quickly, some slowly, some never; it probably follows the same curve of probability as did the marbles.

Insight provides another joy of teaching. To have a student suddenly grin with delight is a delight in itself.

*　　　*　　　*

When Mary Goette wanted to interest her political science class in politics, she would ask them to write a brief history of the family's political behavior. What did your father say about elections? What did your mother say? Did they vote? How did they vote? How has that affected your political beliefs? Most of them followed their parents, because that was the "right" way.

The next step would be to discuss the issues and then to find out the platforms of each party.

Underneath any platform lay a whole set of assumptions about human nature, about crime and punishment, about work and laziness, about the role of government, about the evils of foreign ideas.

Goette's job was to help her students understand the issues and to help them discover the hidden assumptions behind each party's platform.

Only after the students grasped some of these complexities would she invite partisan speakers in during an election campaign. By then, the students were prepared to ask the critical question, to uncover how well or ill the candidate was prepared to vote as a representative.

More than that, she urged every student to volunteer as a worker in a campaign, to get involved with whichever party attracted the student. Each student was urged to attend the party caucus and to introduce a resolution as part of a platform. It was a laboratory experience; it led to great insight.

*   *   *

A Christmas gift book brought me a new insight.

It is not only college freshmen who must relearn their mental patterns and revise their structure to conform to a wider view of the world. Mature, well-trained, competent scientists, often eminent in their field, occasionally must restructure their thinking. And that is not easy.

Stephen Jay Gould, the paleontologist from Harvard who has written columns for *Natural History* as well as about ten books in a style that the rest of us can read, has documented in careful detail one such case. In *Wonderful Life,* Gould (1989) tells us the story of Charles Doolittle Walcott, who discovered the very ancient Burgess shale in the Canadian Rockies. It contained fossilized bodies of hundreds of very early animals, a precious record of the Cambrian explosion of diverse life forms over 500 million years ago— almost the oldest fossils known.

Gould's major point, one that he stresses over and over again, is that Walcott, the top paleontologist in America, squeezed these animal forms into a classification system based on modern surviving forms. Walcott assumed that these were simpler forms, antecedent to those living today, and thus ancestral to the insects and crawfish and worms with which we are familiar. They were different, however, and the attempt to squeeze them into the wrong taxonomic box Gould called "shoehorning."

Many years later, other scientists, notably Henry Whittington, Derek Briggs, and Simon Conway Morris, reexamined the fossil-bearing shale, met trouble, reexamined and compared, and finally reported that the Burgess fossils simply did not fit into the prevailing phyla. They represented new and unknown phyla, which the scientists then named. Thus, they literally created new patterns because the old taxonomies were inadequate.

In creating the new patterns of taxonomy, they also upset the traditional scheme of evolutionary development. For years, the diagrams in the books showed simple life getting more and more complex and branching out into more and more species. Some of the species did not survive in the struggle for living space, and some were lost when the climate changed, but most scientists thought in terms of a cone of increasing diversity.

According to Gould, the Burgess shale modifies this conception by revealing that the greatest diversity occurred early on, in the great Cambrian explosion of life forms. From then on, for reasons unknown, many of these life forms disappeared. The mental pattern of the cone did not fit and had to be reexamined, says Gould.

Wonderful Life is too rich and rewarding to be dismissed in these few paragraphs, especially by this writer, who has trouble even pronouncing the names of the strange and wonderful species that once lived in the antique ocean and died off to disappear forever, leaving behind a few rare fossil footprints to remind us of the contingent nature of history.

With a little change of luck, things would have been altogether different, and we would never have evolved and would never have wondered about life and love and the stars and the nature of human nature and teaching by inquiry. With a little bit of luck, we did evolve, and we can wonder and dream and inquire. I'm glad.

That was a nice Christmas gift. Thank you, David.

*   *   *

October 18, 1990

Dear Walter,

Your additional chapters have arrived and have been read with eagerness; now they are being read again with greater curiosity and attention than before; it happened in this manner.

Our chairman, Bob Wallace, the senior history professor here, heard me mention your manuscript and asked about it, with the consequence that he borrowed it and read it and told me how delighted he was. It seems that you have described in words just about how he has been teaching for years; the delight he expressed has persuaded me to read the whole set of chapters over again.

According to Bob, since the method of inquiry is the way he was taught, it is also the way in which he teaches. "I didn't know there was any other way nearly as good" were his words. So if a fellow like Bob, so universally respected here, has been teaching by inquiry, it needs must follow that I pay closer attention to what you are arguing. As a consequence, every chapter you sent me I am now rereading.

After our discussion last night in which he told me that he would write to you expressing his feelings, he called me in this morning to show me some of the problems he has used in history classes: problems of eyewitness reports, problems of conflicts of opinions, problems of variant interpretations. He lets freshmen tackle these in order to develop the skills needed. Rather than lecture on all these skills, as I have done, he dumps the students into problems and lets them learn. More than that, he was delighted to read about Perry's scheme, something he had never heard of before. Black-and-white thinking is characteristic of freshmen, Bob says, and it is part of our job to make them realize that most issues end up in grays and that choosing between grays becomes dependent on subtle choices and often our biases. He agreed with you on so many things that I am still a bit staggered. He even said that helping students to mature was one of the major functions of a college. I thought that all I needed to know in order to teach was a lot of history.

*No cross blazed in the night sky as that which con-
verted Constantine; no epiphany occurred while I was
walking on the road to Damascus; the balance of persuasion was tipped when two people whom I respect
presented the same arguments.*

*Now I really have work to do; Bob has shown me how
to organize classes with tension in the learning process, and at the same time I am reading your chapters
over again to find his same argument in different language. Reading them over again permits me to glean
other insights as well. Thank you for the opportunity.*

*The manuscript shall be returned with marginal notes,
some of which I shall erase, as soon as two other
teachers have read it.*

*Another comment from Bob: Most of us can learn to
read some pretty murky prose, but it takes an effort.
When we can read the same ideas in clear language,
it is much easier and more pleasant. Therefore, I am
also trying to write shorter sentences and clearer
prose. "Easy reading is hard writing," Bob said.*

*Do you have many more chapters to come? Have you
interested a publisher yet?*

*It's great so far. Let us have more. How's that for short
and clear?*

Historically,

Jack

13

Innocents Abroad: A Case of Inquiry

"Aren't you afraid of getting shot in Nicaragua?

"Nicaragua? Is that part of Mexico?"

"Well, at least you'll be safe in Honduras. We have our National Guard down there, don't we?"

"Is that south of the equator? Will it be winter?"

Some of our friends were even more ignorant about the geography and politics of Central America than we were.

In May of 1989 my wife signed up for a study tour in Central America offered by the Center for Global Education at Augsburg College, a Lutheran institution with a commitment to global understanding. Undecided about going, I tagged along to Sue's first briefing for the trip.

We met Professor Jan Mathison, who started us right off with a brief problem in studying maps. Around the room she had hung a Mercator projection map, a polar projection map, a Peters, a Goode, and various other attempts at map making, ranging on to a MacArthur map, which positioned north at the bottom and placed Australia at the top, colored more brightly than any of the rest of the world, which was now "down under," less conspicuous, and strangely upside down.

We wandered about noticing the differences and chuckling at the different perspectives and realizing suddenly how comfortably we had accepted North America as properly at the Center of the World. We laughed uneasily at the naivete of our own ethnocentrism, our unconscious acceptance of our cultural assumptions and the way we draw maps. Even the standard old Mercator map has the midline equator way south of center.

When Jan next gave us two conflicting news articles on the same event and asked us to explain how that could have happened, it hit me. She was giving us facts and asking us to generalize; she was giving us conflicting views and asking us to explain and to judge. She wanted us to discover. She was teaching by inquiry.

An hour later, I wrote a check for eighteen hundred and five dollars to become the eleventh member of the study group. The youngest was twenty, most were in their thirties or forties, and two of us were over seventy.

*   *   *

But Jan had a different name for this teaching; she called it the Circle of Praxis and briefly explained how a Brazilian educator named Paulo Freire had used the system to educate peasants into developing a different view of their place in the world. When coupled with liberation theology, which justified the empowerment of the poor, this led to considerable social change, which was not welcomed by the established institutions of church and state.

The Circle of Praxis involved taking a closer look at part of the society, reflecting on it in discussions, revising your own opinions, doing this over and over again, and gradually coming up with a world view closer to the observed facts. The circle involved alternating periods of observation and reflection and discussion.

"That is the method we shall use on this study tour. We shall examine our beliefs, then expose ourselves to several interviews of different people, and then discuss and reflect on what we have learned. Then immerse ourselves once more into the group we are studying, and gather more facts, followed by more reflection."

But first we were to read some of the history of Central America and relearn Spanish and generally cram two or three months of study into a couple of weeks.

When you want to learn, you remember a lot.

*   *   *

Certain questions kept surfacing. We struggled trying to find answers in Honduras.

Did U.S. aid help the poor people of Honduras?

If the Hondurans liked us so much, why had mobs attacked and burned the U.S. Embassy?

If Honduras was the showplace for the type of democracy that the United States fostered in Central America, how well was that democracy working?

*   *   *

We saw no U.S. National Guard troops in Honduras; instead, we saw young Honduran soldiers carrying rifles at the airport and on almost every street in Tegucigalpa, the capital city. The night we arrived, a Honduran student leader was assassinated. Two days later, a union leader was assassinated. The following day, another union leader was assassinated. All three of them had been openly critical of the U.S. presence and U.S. support of the contras on Honduran soil.

We interviewed Anibal Puerto, who collected reports on such assassinations and on arrest and torture of citizens for the Human Rights Committee of Honduras. He blamed the death squads of the army. Puerto had been bombed and had been threatened with death.

We visited a Christian Committee for Development, funded by foreign churches, which tried to improve the literacy and health and farming techniques of the campesinos. They took us out to a goat farm, where miserably poor people struggled on rocky soil to grow a few crops in a season of drought.

We listened to a history professor give us a brief history of Honduras and also tell us of the impact of U.S. corporations, particularly the fruit companies, which paid few taxes.

On we went to the Central Committee for the National Party, the conservatives who opposed the Liberals currently in power. (In November, they did win the election.) We talked with the adult education director, with a school principal, with schoolteachers, and with schoolchildren in one classroom with no windows and no electric lights. When we exchanged questions, one little girl asked us, "Do you have lots of crises in your country?"

We interviewed agrarian reformers who struggled to use the law that gave unused land to the campesinos. After failing to get the law respected, they would squat on the land to claim it. Several such groups had been driven off by soldiers using weapons supplied by the United States. We visited the squatters and saw the ruined farms. A helicopter whirled overhead.

We visited the U.S. embassy, hearing the official policy as to how much good the Americans were doing. Then, since we did not challenge them, we heard other stories of how inept and brutal the Honduran police were, how corrupt the judges were, how it was a struggle to audit the books recording how AID money was spent.

We visited the Honduran congress and were conducted about by a delegate from the National party, who had our names read into the record as "prominent intellectuals from the United States."

We visited the United Nations High Commission for Refugees to learn about the many groups surviving in camps in Honduras. Some had fled south from Guatemala, afraid of the genocide there (carried out by the government that the CIA had installed). Some had fled from El Salvador and its brutal war between the guerrillas and the army supplied with U.S. weapons. Some had fled north from Nicaragua and lived in camps along the border. Here they lived on the supplies from the United States, making periodic raids into Nicaragua to keep the war there going.

Then we listened to the presidential candidate of the small Christian Socialist Party, whose platform included land reform and taxation of the foreign corporations and stopping the U.S. presence in Honduras and getting rid of the contras and making peace with El Salvador and working with the Central American Parliament to establish peace and justice.

And we also stopped to discuss what we had learned and to reflect on the great diversity of views and to wonder which was the more accurate or the more believable. My notebook was filling up rapidly.

One night, our youngest member was stopped by three police with rifles. They frisked him and took his passport but were unable to read it. Also that night, the third critic of government policy was murdered.

*   *   *

We were collecting many points of view; we were examining our own prejudgments; we were challenging each other's interpretations. And we were trying to judge others' views as compared with their place in society. We were learning by inquiry. Also, we were doing what any good reporter does, getting lots of different opinions.

In five days, this had become a far more exciting trip than looking at old cathedrals and buying quaint stuff in the markets.

*   *   *

When we flew south over the border into Nicaragua, we fully expected to see a nation at war. We saw plenty of destruction, most of it from the earthquake of 1972. When money was sent to the dictator Somoza to help the reconstruction, he squirreled it away in his Swiss bank accounts. The ruins remained.

As we began talking with Nicaraguans, certain questions were uppermost in my mind.

Were the Sandinistas actually Communists, as our government labeled them?

Why was the economy so miserable? Was it because of Sandinista incompetence, or was it because of the embargo by the United States and the burden of the eight years of contra war?

What were the contras like? Were they supported and befriended by the Nicaraguan people, or would they collapse if United States aid were withdrawn? Did they actually commit acts of terrorism? Were they still raiding villages during the cease-fire?

What would happen in the national election of February 1990? Would it be fairly conducted? Would the losers accept the outcome?

What did the rest of the world think about the Sandinistas and their eight-year struggle against the United States?

Often I felt as though I were one of my own students doing an ethnography.

*   *   *

We saw few weapons until the night we left our house to walk down the street to an ice-cream shop. As we passed the modest house of President Daniel Ortega, Jan called out "Buenas noches" to the two soldiers on guard duty. They responded, "Buenas noches," and then we noticed their rifles.

Our first interview was with Cesar Vivas, editor of *La Prensa*, the opposition newspaper, extremely critical of the Sandinista government. The Chamorro family, which owned the paper, had joined the Sandinistas to help overthrow the Somoza government. Then they split over policy and led the opposition. Vivas was hopeful about the 1990 election. "The opposition must unite on one candidate. All other parties oppose the Sandinistas. Even the Socialists and the Communist party oppose the Sandinistas. All they know is war. They are not Communists; they are militarists." He also thought that his publisher, Violeta Chamorro, would make a strong candidate. Vivas opposed the U.S. embargo on trade because it hurt everyone.

When we asked whether he had received CIA money, he replied, "There is no proof."

Then we met with the head of the small Christian Socialist party, which also opposed the Sandinistas. They urge peaceful, nonviolent measures, although they are proud of having joined in the revolution against the last Somoza, the third member of that much-hated family, which had been installed and supported with U.S. help. Their party wanted no more outside intervention. "Democracy is not given; it is achieved."

And that same day, our first full day in Nicaragua, we met with a group of women at Barrio Batahola, the first communal housing project for the landless. Since the government quickly ran out of money, it remains the only such project. We met in a school, spotlessly clean and neat, with women who were learning to read and to write and to use typewriters and sewing machines and to improve their cooking skills and health. Their husbands had initially objected to their attending school. When their meals improved, they wanted to join as well. "We were strong," one woman grinned. They supported the Sandinistas with enthusiasm. Their life had vastly improved.

Next morning, a Baptist missionary tried to explain liberation theology to us, asserting that it worked out to be generally anticapitalist, anti-imperialist, and anti-exploitation. He said that most of the American Baptists opposed the Reagan war against Nicaragua.

The Sandinistas took their name from the rebel leader Sandino, who fought against the twenty-year occupation by the U.S. Marines in the 1930s. When the Marines left, after establishing Somoza as the ruler, Somoza made peace with Sandino. They had a victory banquet and signed a treaty. As Sandino left, he was murdered. Somoza and his sons formed a brutal dictatorship for the next forty-six years, with U.S. help.

Our prize that day was Dr. Rudolfo Sandino, lawyer, justice, professor, and now on the Supreme Electoral Council, set up to ensure a fair election. He was not related at all to the famous freedom leader Sandino.

The council has five members. Two are from the ruling Sandinista party, two are from the opposition, and the fifth is a neutral acceptable to both, Dr. Sandino.

He explained the machinery that they were installing for an honest election: printing ID cards with a photo for each registered voter, training many election judges, training overseers, allowing many foreign observers in, and maintaining a careful control over the ballots. "I have faith in pure technical strategies," Dr. Sandino told us. The cost of setting up the election machinery was paid for largely by $25 million from Scandinavian countries, plus teams of experts from Germany, France, Canada, and Spain.

I began glimpsing some answers to those questions about Nicaragua buzzing in my head.

*   *   *

We met a Sandinista, a bright, attractive woman with dark eyes and a forceful manner of speaking. She had been elected to the congress and was also studying to be a lawyer. During the revolution, her house had been bombed by Somoza's forces while she and her baby were inside.

Why is the economy so poor? "There are two reasons," Señora Angela Rosa told us. "One is that the government has made too many mistakes. The other is that the United States is bleeding us with their contra war and blocking our trade with their illegal embargo. Yes, we have made mistakes, but the war and the embargo hurt us more.

"The United States owes us money," she told us. "We took our case to the World Court and we won and they refuse to pay. And they call us dishonest."

"And what mistakes did the Sandinistas make?" we asked.

"The worst was attacking the Miskito Indians. We were wrong. Now we are giving them autonomy and letting them make many decisions on their own."

It was a busy day. We visited a museum of *alfabetización*, which is a wonderful name for literacy. The small building records the strenuous attempt by the Sandinistas to send young volunteers to the countryside to teach adults to read and to write.

And we heard from a bearded young missionary who told of his training young men as foresters only to have many killed by the contras. Despite the cease-fire, the contras were still making terrorist raids, still killing health workers, teachers, and any trained leaders, and still being supplied by air-drop by the CIA.

On our way to Chinandega for an overnight visit with local families, we picked up hitchhikers and tried to learn more from them. One woman proudly told us that she was a Conservative and would vote against the Sandinistas just as she had voted against Somoza. Two nurses avoided political issues. Instead, they talked of the high infant death rate and the lack of medicine.

The cooperative farm we visited was owned and worked by eleven men and one woman. It was part of the 25 percent of the Nicaraguan land in co-ops. Proudly they showed us about their fields with the crops suffering from the drought. We took photos with our expensive Japanese cameras. Then they told us that they needed a water pump and asked whether we could give them one. They had taken half a day off from work for us, what did we have for them?

All we had for them was a look of embarrassment. Our leaders had specifically told us not to do the charity act, not to think that basic social inequalities can be cured by a quick fix of a gift.

On to meet with the local leaders of the Conservative Popular

Alliance, who hoped that all of the anti-Sandinista parties would unite around one candidate. They mocked the literacy campaign. They mocked the Sandinistas as inept leaders. "They are not Communists, they are opportunists." They blamed the American Democrats for giving the world to the Russians. "Do you all contribute money to your party?" we asked. They responded with shock. "No, we work hard for our money." Next we asked who gives the orders in the party. "Orders come from above. This is democracy. It is voluntary." They liked the contras. They fantasized about the glorious day when the U.S. Marines would march in to set their world right side up once more.

That evening, thirty of us sat in a circle under the huge trees in the walled-in garden behind a church. In the dusk, eighteen women from Chinandega told us of their lives and and their hopes. One had learned to read during the literacy campaign. "I kept on in school and have now finished the fourth grade." Proudly she sat straight as we all clapped. Another had just finished the sixth grade and was soon to become a teacher. We clapped even louder. I wondered whether our Conservative party friends who had mocked the literacy campaign had ever talked to such women.

Liberation theology was the moving spirit of the group, which was led by a Dominican priest. When he began talking and would not stop, I wondered how well he could liberate women if the one man did all the talking. The priest also told the story of the World Court and the victory by the Nicaraguans against the United States and then the walkout by the United States. Somehow, our home newspapers seemed to have ignored that story.

More and more interviews. My notes piled up. We were still seeking a pattern to make sense of all the conflicting opinions. Finally, I found a pattern that helped.

After the Vietnam War, our army decided to avoid such a costly bloodletting on a foreign soil where the odds were against our winning. Instead they developed the policy of LIW, or low-intensity warfare.

LIW saves us money, the policy argues. Compared to high-intensity warfare using nuclear bombs or medium-intensity warfare using conventional weapons and sending our own troops, low-intensity warfare is much cheaper.

We commit no troops. Instead, we send weapons and bullets and encourage partisan groups to fight their government with terrorism or sabotage. If that does not work, we impose trade restrictions to starve the stubborn people into submission. If that does not work, we threaten invasion and make the small country waste money and labor in preparing to resist an invasion that may never come. All the while, the American public is "disinformed" by official reports and name-calling. The most frequent names are Communist and Drug Trafficker. Dissident groups receive secret money from the CIA; neighboring countries are encouraged to block trade with the target community or risk losing their aid.

This policy is printed in army manuals; it is used; it teaches the world what the United States really does when we talk about "fostering democracy." It scares me.

In January of 1990, the army issued a revision of its policy, entitled "Military Operations in Low Intensity Conflict." The press summary made it sound utterly in violation of our own Constitution, in violation of the United Nations Charter, and in violation of the charter of the Organization of American States, which forbids armed intervention in other signatory states.

Seeing our government's behavior in Honduras and in Nicaragua as part of low-intensity warfare suddenly made sense of the suspicions that my own government was disinforming me about the contras, about the Sandinistas, about the people in Honduras, about the government in El Salvador.

Seeing the support for Nicaragua from Europe and Canada also made sense. Our allies were not accepting our brutal and cynical treatment of the Central Americans.

Two weeks do not an expert make. But two weeks in Central America did make one disillusioned citizen wonder why we don't honestly face up to the need for land reform, help our neighbors to include all citizens in owning land and thus secure a stake in capitalism and democratic government. Then we should get out of the way and let them make their own decisions, some of which will be mistakes, the very essence of freedom.

That would be even cheaper than low-intensity warfare, more honest, and truer to the values we proclaim.

*   *   *

It was an experience, a real learning experience, the kind that I had tried to create in small for years. It was adult experiential learning. We had gathered data. We had interviewed people of many different positions and politics and interests. We had felt the discomfort of readjusting our mental patterns. We had formed and asked our own questions and noted the clarity of the response or the avoidance of any response. We had discussed these answers and argued among our little group of eleven.

The eleven of us did not agree on everything. And we knew that our information was often meager.

What else would we want to know?

More about the Sandinistas and their plans for the economy. More about why the Sandinistas deal with Cuba and the Soviets. More about the effects of the embargo. More about the contra leadership. More about the low-intensity warfare plans. More about the apparent manipulation of news by our War Department. Suddenly we were hungry for news, eager to look for Central American items in the newspaper.

Teaching by inquiry does that to you. It arouses curiosity and a continuing eagerness to learn more.

Even for old people.

QUESTION THREE

HOW CAN YOU START?

Chapters Fourteen and Fifteen recapitulate the skills that the teacher needs to teach inductively and stress the collecting of data from many viewpoints.

The final chapter warns you of some of the risks involved in challenging students, promises parents some benefits, and promises the teacher some rewards and delights.

14

Changing Your Role as a Teacher

This chapter is written for those teachers who are attracted to teaching by inquiry but are still reluctant to try it. Although most of my examples come from college teaching, the method works well in high school and is probably already used far more there than in college.

This chapter pulls together the comments pertinent to the teacher's role, what you say in class and how you organize a lesson.

Give It a Try

Now I know very well that some of you are superb at lecturing. I have heard you. You enter a classroom with dignity blended with friendliness; you are well organized; you speak clearly; you make your points well; and you buttress them with plenty of factual evidence. Here and there is a sly joke for the subtle students, and here and there is a bolder one for the less subtle students. And your jokes advance the point you are making; they are not irrelevant gags for the sake of giggles. You pace your delivery; you know how long the period is, and you finish on time. You know from long experience that nothing is ever learned after the bell.

You know far more than the text, more than is in your notes or in your lectures. You know an awful lot and can field questions deftly and factually and provide a really eager student with an author or two for more data.

And you are courteous to other teachers; you never keep a class overtime. You use the blackboard skillfully to indicate the outline of the argument or to spell a difficult term or to sketch. And at the end of the period, you erase the board, leaving it clean for the next teacher.

If you recognized yourself here, please do not discard these magnificent skills and your friendly personality traits. No, I am asking you to expand the opportunities for those bright students in front of you to learn more of the process of learning. I am asking you to let them use their mental skills to learn the professional skills of your discipline. Help them to forge new mental patterns while breaking the crust of a few remaining childish patterns. They might become more like you.

One way is that mentioned in Chapter One. There, the lecturer deliberately gave an alternative theory to that given by the text and thus forced the students to compare the two and to make some judgment. More than that, he did not warn that he was going to lecture on Charles Beard, whose views on the Constitution were certainly controversial. He just did it. He let the students discover and wince and become uncomfortable until they interrupted to ask questions.

The cold war with its exaggerated Americanism and paranoid fear of critical ideas began right after the end of World War II. My career in college teaching began at the same time; not the most propitious period for encouraging critical thinking. Yet such a marvelous opportunity.

Avoid controversy was the usual advice. If you wish to keep your job, don't rattle your cage. The typical response is to be bland and smooth and buttery. Offend no one. But there is another way, and that is to assume that every student wishes to learn some sort of knowledge that will stand scrutiny. If, in this process, some feelings are offended, that may just contribute to the learning process.

That irritation may well be the trigger that gets a student started to prove a point. Along the way, a student may learn a lot about proving points. The student will also learn about using historical sources, and learn that other students have been taught very different slants on history.

Frustration is often needed to jar a person out of a mental rut.

Look back at the theoretical considerations expressed in Chapter Three. Remember when Chet Meyers (1986, p. 32) pointed out that "The most important aspect of this part of the learning cycle is the creation of an atmosphere in which probing, puzzling, and raising questions provide a natural challenge to the students' present mental structures, thereby creating the disequilibrium necessary for change."

As Carl Westphal, a psychologist who tried to teach me how to counsel other old folks in an Elder Network, once put it, "Your job is to get them to see alternatives and to make choices of ways that are less self-destructive or less isolating. Alcoholics must learn to quit boozing; smokers may need to quit smoking; overeaters must learn to eat less; isolates must learn to phone their old friends."

> "As long as you do what you've always done,
> you're gonna get what you've always got."

When a lecturer realizes that half of the class does not take notes on his or her magnificent productions, and half of those who do take notes write them poorly, that teacher ought to be frustrated. Frustration opens the door to change with teachers as well as with students. We are trying to get students into the fourth level that Piaget described. Several times I've quoted Chet Meyers, who teaches in Minneapolis and encourages students to interact, to think, to respond, to criticize. "Lecturing is obviously a very comfortable mode of teaching, as witness its long tradition and continued predominance. After all, monologue is less risky than dialogue" (Meyers, 1986, p. 57). Then he points out that most lecturers allow no time for interaction, allow no time for challenging assumptions, allow no time for students to process the material. Just write your notes, and write fast.

You great lecturers who wish to experiment with inquiry can do it in several easy steps.

Three Easy Steps

1. Create tension. You can rebuild a few of those magnificently tooled lectures into messages that create some tension. Trim

your lecture shorter and deliberately contradict the textbook, or government policy, or a previous lecture.

2. Ask students for opinions. I do not mean pausing briefly, "Are there any questions?" and then racing on. The only question you usually get is "Will this be on the test?"

No. Ask students whether they agree with what you have said. And then, whatever their response, shift to another student for judgment. "Do you agree with her?"

Or inquire: "Have you heard any contrary views? Where?" Drag out of somebody that the textbook disagrees with you; that the country is divided on the issue; or that not enough is known yet to be sure.

3. Take time. Should this be your first attempt, students will be wary. They need encouragement to disagree with a teacher's views; they need practice in speaking up; they need reassurance that they won't get walloped for showing doubts. All of those suspicions took a long time to develop, and their hesitation is a terrible commentary on most of our educational practice. Many teachers simply do not permit disagreement, do not encourage disagreement, do not provoke discussion over meaningful issues.

During the cold war, one Texas school board issued a ruling on high school debates: Students may debate, but not over controversial issues.

Most of us still look on the rows of students as empty buckets waiting eagerly to be filled by the fountain of wisdom up front. You are paid to spout, and you refuse to cheat the taxpayer. You spout. Tell them only the truth, and have them memorize it; this we call education.

But the truth as you know truth may change. Soon your students may live in a far different world, with new issues, new terms, new conflicts. We must prepare those students to do their own thinking, to learn to question the assumptions of a speaker, to learn to seek for alternative answers, and most of all to learn to ask questions, real questions about the nature of evidence and the nature of proof and how you know for sure what you think you know for sure.

First Try

So you are actually brave enough to try one class of teaching by inquiry. You prepare for the big day. You have a problem ready to start the class.

You pose that problem. You wait for an answer. Three seconds later, you begin to panic. Your hands sweat. The class just stares at you dumbly.

Calm down. Students need time to think. They need time to digest the very notion that you actually want them to think. They need time to figure out what the question meant and also whether they dare stick their necks out.

Wait.

Smile. Don't even glance at your wristwatch.

Stare expectantly at one or two students that you normally count on to be ready. Nudge them a little with your smile.

Wait. Don't say a word.

Smile expectantly.

Wait.

In two or three hours, someone will offer a tentative response. Should you be able to sneak a glance at the time, you will find that those two hours were really about forty seconds.

Glory be, the student who speaks up gives the "correct" response right out of the text. In sheer gratitude, you want to shout: "Good for you. That's right. I knew that I could count on you."

Don't you dare. Don't you dare tell that student that the answer is right. Don't you dare deny the class the fun of thinking and deciding and judging.

Instead, you turn and lay that delight on some other student. "Do you agree with that?"

Shock. Many students have never been asked that. Another commentary on our system.

The students will survive. You will live through it. With a bit of patience and practice, both you and the students will learn to discuss an issue, to question an assumption, to define a word, to explore alternatives, to gain the skills needed for thinking. Since you already know how to do this, your job is to learn to be quiet.

This takes time and many repetitions. The students will learn; and if you are half as smart as I think you are, you will learn as well. Laryngitis helps.

Lost in Fog

But some students have sat through many discussions and have learned all sorts of ways to create fog: that wordy, mushy, vague sort of word-slinging that sounds almost intelligent. When the fog rolls in, the teacher must listen carefully and then ask what one certain key term means and then ask another student whether that is an adequate answer. Thus you regain control and keep the class away from the fog artists. Soon the class will learn to challenge a fog machine. Remember Hemingway's one priceless quality for a good writer: "to have a built-in, shock-proof crap-detector."

Many of the problems in a class arise over defining terms. One simple method of clarifying a term is to ask for some examples. Semanticists may refer to this as "going down the semantic ladder" to a fact or to an observation.

Fog artists go up the ladder to more abstract terms.

Unfortunately, the fog machines have been rewarded in the past. Some teachers permit discussions, aimless, rambling discussions that have no goal and no beginning and no end. After all, they do fill the hour and thus kill the hour.

If your class threatens to degenerate into fog, try a quick home remedy.

"The question we began with was ———. Since you all seem content to shift away from that question, we must have answered it to your satisfaction. So, before we turn to another topic, will you all write down your answer in your notes. In two minutes one of you can read the answer."

Wait a respectable few moments and ask a student to read the answer. And then begin again: "Do you agree with that?"

When you have been derailed, you must get the train back on the track.

Although I keep warning the teacher not to talk, by no means should the teacher lose control. Classes seldom get very far by themselves; someone leads.

Data First

A crucial preparation by the teacher involves organizing material to provoke discussion, to provide data, and to present alternative views.

That is so important a part of your job that the next chapter is devoted to it. For now, let me assume that you have collected some material.

Here is one way. You have several examples of a well-known and often-quoted notion in sociology. Normally you would give a lecture, you would explain the concept in abstract terms, and then you would trot out your examples to illustrate and prove it.

Just for today, just for fun, and just for the experience, let us reverse that procedure.

Give the examples first.

Do not state the key concept at all.

Let the students generalize about the process going on in the examples.

Let them decide on the concept; they might even invent a far better label than the traditional label. Here is such a case.

First example. Your first day in high school, you attend a class and the teacher calls out the roll of names, recognizes your name, and says:

"Did you have an older sister named Eileen?"

Embarrassed, you confess that, yes, you did.

"Oh, that's marvelous. I know that you are going to be just as smart as she was. Eileen was an excellent student, always getting high grades."

And somehow your grades are pretty good in that class. And somehow you find yourself studying harder for that class. And somehow the teacher keeps praising you. And somehow your grades get even better.

Second example. Your first day in high school, you attend a class and the teacher calls out the roll of names, recognizes your name, and says:

"Did you have an older sister named Eileen?"

Embarrassed, you confess that, yes, you did once have such a sister.

"Well, I remember her very distinctly. And if you think that you can get away with any of the tricks she pulled, you have another think coming. I will not stand for it, and I will be keeping my eye on you. Do you follow me? Speak up. I can't hear you mumble. Speak up."

And somehow that class doesn't go very well for you. Whatever happens, you find that some of the blame falls on you. The teacher moves you to a front seat "to keep an eye on you," and more blame seems to fall on you. Your resentment grows so bitter that you seldom study for that class, and your responses become worse and worse. Your grades get lower and lower.

Third example: You are out hanging around with some friends one summer evening when you see a parked car with the keys in it. Impulsively on a dare, you all borrow the car for a brief joyride. You all take turns driving. The last to drive is the youngest and least skilled, who crashes the car into another. The police arrest the gang.

Your father is angry, but he can afford to hire a lawyer, who gets you off. Not so Len, the last one driving. He gets a stiff fine and his name in the paper.

Your parents insist that you stay away from Len, who is a bad influence because he got you into all that trouble. After all, you have a college career ahead of you. Your other buddies also get the message to dump Len. Len seeks out other friends; two months later, his name again appears in the court records. This time he loses his job because he sits for ten days in the jail.

When you are a sophomore in college, you read

in your hometown paper that Len has been sent up for a more serious charge and is spending a year in prison.

You know that Len was no good from the beginning.

Fourth example: Several teachers were told by a research psychologist that certain pupils in their new classes were ripe to become excellent students who would astonish the teacher. The researcher obligingly gave the teachers their names.

In actuality, these selected students were perfectly normal, average kids who had no special abilities and no particular promise. However, the teachers now believed that they were special. Their grades went up; their performance improved; even their IQ test scores went up.

The expectations of the teachers were met. Other students in the class did not improve nearly as much. You may recognize this as the Rosenthal and Jacobsen study in 1968.

You have given these four examples to your class. In this case, it might be best to have them typed and duplicated so that each student can compare all of the examples and read them again.

Several options are open to you. You might ask the whole class to look for common elements. You might ask students to sit in groups of two and find common elements and try to describe the social process going on. Using small groups ensures that even the shy kids get a chance to speak up. It also means that they make some sort of commitment to a decision.

Then ask two groups to merge and agree on their answers. The shy ones who have reached some conclusion now may find that they must defend their position. It is much easier to do that in a small group.

A class will discover all sorts of social processes going on in these four cases. Labeling is the first and most obvious. Then there are the effects of labeling on the victim and on those in power. Then there is the incremental effect as the label gets reinforced, with more people accepting it. Then there is the use of power to create conditions that make the label come true and thus justify the label in a circular reinforcement.

You might ask the class to recall similar examples from their own histories. Many will. If some miss the point and wander afield, use the class to tether them to the data.

When the process is clear, ask them to invent a name for this concept. They may invent more descriptive names than "self-fulfilling prophecy" or "Pygmalion effect" or "Rosenthal effect," which are already used.

When they are through, they should have the examples, their notes describing the process, and finally the various names that the class invented. And if someone in the class recognizes that this process is similar to that of the logical organization of an essay (as distinct from the pyramid style), then you have a student with insight.

Congratulations. You have just led a class in discovery. You have demonstrated your confidence in their ability.

A Look Back

1. Start with data. Present the students with facts that pose some problem of meaning or of contradiction or of puzzlement. Or if this is a brief period before a lecture, start with a brief problem and ask for tentative answers.

2. Encourage discussion and give the students time to think and silence to think in.

3. Stand aside. Let them solve problems and correct each other and work it out.

4. Let them work in pairs and then in fours to involve the quiet ones.

5. Get them to test their generalizations against other data.

6. Get them to look for additional data to deny or confirm what you brought in.

7. Rearrange the seating to encourage talk if the discussion will be long.

8. Review your own attitude and manner for acceptance of

student opinion. Show your willingness to listen and to respect the student.

*   *   *

Now let's take a look at collecting and organizing material for inquiry teaching. That needs its own chapter.

15

Organizing
Your Materials

In the last chapter, we organized a simple lesson around Rosenthal's famous experiment. We presented four examples, and then the discussion followed. Out of the cases, the class generated some commonalities and described the social process.

So you are ready for more, perhaps a lesson that takes two or three days. That takes preparation. Start long in advance.

First: Select the problem; it usually grows out of the data in the text or the previous lessons.

Second: Collect data. Keep file folders marked to drop in a new clipping when you find it. Do it now, do it regularly, because next month you will never remember that great article you read in August, or was it May? Whenever you find a book that looks useful, make a bibliography slip for it. If it is not useful, make a bibliography slip anyway so that next time you won't waste much time over that book.

One of my professors once advised me, "Make a bib slip on everything you read, whether or not you finish the book or whether or not you like the book. It will save you hours of searching later."

The stress on data is because of the rule of *evidence first*. Remember my walk in the woods with the botanist, Dr. Gray? He made us look carefully before we attached any labels. Most of the teachers I have quoted here followed that rule. First you look and collect data, and then, after study, you generate the concepts and generalizations.

Whether it was Bill Walton teaching probability step by step with one marble or Mary Goette having students examine their own families for voting histories or Jerry Tammen with the contaminated water supplies, each first had students look at data.

And remember the Rosenthal effect? In that case, the person in power attached the label without looking at the data and thus may have victimized a student. Get the evidence before attaching any labels.

Hanged by the Neck

Below are some examples of data. Some are quotations, some are tables of figures. Your problem is the use of the death penalty. The general question is: Does the death penalty deter other people from committing murder?

When J. Edgar Hoover, director of the FBI, wanted to argue for the death penalty for murderers, here is what he had to say: "Who in all good conscience can say that Julius and Ethel Rosenberg, the spies who delivered the secret of the atomic bomb into the hands of the Soviets, should have been spared when their treachery caused the shadow of annihilation to fall upon all of the world's peoples?"

Examples are persuasive. Hoover also brought up this case: "What would have been the chances of rehabilitating Jack Gilbert Graham, who placed a bomb in his own mother's luggage and blasted her and forty-three other innocent victims into oblivion as they rode an airliner across a peaceful sky?"

And one more from Hoover. "Was not this small, blonde, six-year-old girl a child of God? She was choked, beaten, and raped by a sex fiend whose pregnant wife reportedly helped him lure the innocent child into his car and who sat and watched the assault on the screaming youngster. . . . the time-proven deterrents to crime are sure detection, swift apprehension, and proper punishment."

Okay, now you are going to set up a lesson on capital punishment and whether it deters murders. Those three quotations above could make a good beginning. They have shock value; they come from an authority; they are brief and clearly stated.

A few teachers stop there. They already have the voice of

authority. They have the popular viewpoint and some simple psychology. They know that they themselves do not commit murders because they are afraid of being hanged or shot or fried; capital punishment obviously deters them.

The question is whether capital punishment will deter someone else from committing a murder. It is not whether capital punishment is an appropriate revenge, if you like revenge. It is not whether it takes the murderer off the street. The question is whether the fear of hanging deters other potential murderers from committing a crime.

Collections of Data

When looking for data and quotations and arguments and examples on such a problem, it is helpful to consult an anthology in which the editor has collected a wide variety of viewpoints. Those Hoover quotations above came from an article reprinted in a book titled *The Death Penalty in America,* edited by Hugo Adam Bedau (1964). That book has all you need for a darned good inquiry session on the question: Does capital punishment deter murderers? It covers all sides of the problem and gives articles long enough for a writer to develop his or her point.

First, you selected your problem.

Second, you collected some data.

Now the third step is to balance your data.

In a more advanced class, you could assign the whole book to be read in a few weeks and then discussed. If all you have are one or two hours of class time, then select a balanced diet, duplicate, and feed the readings to the class one at a time.

Bedau offers "Christian" arguments on both sides. He offers legal arguments on both sides. He offers public opinion polls of the nation and of selected groups, such as prison wardens.

Read this chapter of mine at two levels. It explains how to make up an inductive lesson, and it is such a lesson in itself. Remember that you need balance for the class. And you must encourage students to seek out more data.

To balance the grisly Hoover quotations, try this one:

In 1957, Paul A. Thomas wrote to the wardens of state prisons to ask them three specific questions. Twenty-six of them replied with usable answers (Bedau, 1964, p. 242). Here is a summary.

Question 1. Do you consider capital punishment a deterrent for murder?

26 replies   3 Yes (11%)   23 No (89%)

Question 2. Taking into consideration the state of mind of the offender at the time of the murder, do you think that the offender actually thinks about the consequences which his criminal act might bring upon himself?

26 replies   1 Yes (4%)   24 No (92%)   1 blank

Question 3a. Does the fact that innocent persons have been executed create, in your estimation, a fallacy in the use of capital punishment?

26 replies   16 Yes (62%)   6 No (23%)   4 blank

Question 3b. and is this enough to abolish it in the United States?

26 replies   8 Yes (31%)   14 No (54%)   4 blank

Now wherever you stand on this question, you will see that this chart is going to provoke a discussion. As teacher, all you need do is to present the transparency with the data and ask one student to read the first line, which ought to lead to something like this:

"When twenty-six prison wardens were asked whether they considered capital punishment a deterrent to murder, only 11 percent of them said yes. But 89 percent said no."

If the student does not read it off well, keep trying. Ask another to try, and then a third, to see whether he or she agrees with the second. Never overestimate the ability of students to understand simple statistics. Never overestimate the ability of anyone to read simple statistics.

Class Readiness

Fourth step: Organize a list of the skills your students will need to grasp before they can tackle the data. If they do not know simple statistics, teach them. If they do not know simple arithmetic, teach them.

From then on, it takes its own way. Several times, some strongly opinionated student will object, "Why should we worry about this? It's only opinion. My opinion is as good as the next person's." That should provoke more discussion. And by now, your class ought to be able to distinguish facts from opinions. Facts are verifiable statements. Opinions are personal judgments.

Remember. You are the teacher, not the judge. Just smile and throw each comment into the laps of other students. Never take sides. You are not teaching them the right answer to the problem; you are teaching them how to find a good answer that they can support for reasons that they consider adequate.

Adequate means different things to different people. Those who accept one minister's argument about Christianity may run into a buzz saw of controversy with students who come from a different religious training.

Plus a warning: Religious arguments are usually a no-no in classrooms. Just make sure that neither you nor anybody else indoctrinates. "Can we agree that we disagree on that issue?" is one way to cut off arguments. Or "That appears to be a matter of faith and thus beyond argument, at least in this classroom."

Papers or Transparencies

Fifth: Prepare the materials for the students. Some you duplicate on paper. Some you prepare on transparencies. Some might be on tape or on slides or filmstrips. If you wish to use the same lesson again, don't use much paper.

This next one I usually put on transparencies.

One of the most provocative of Bedau's offerings is Thorsten Sellin's comparative study of states that have capital punishment with those that do not. He gives the homicide rates for Minnesota and Wisconsin (no death penalty) and, alongside them, the rates for

Iowa (death penalty). Sellin's argument is that the three adjoining states have similar people, similar cultural beliefs, and similar educational standards, so that many other variables must be pretty similar.

You have to look at the charts yourself. Briefly, the three states are the same when it comes to homicide rates. It makes no difference to have a death penalty if you are looking for deterrence. The homicide rates are the same.

He repeats the study with Nebraska, North Dakota, and South Dakota. No significant difference.

He repeats the study with Colorado, Missouri, and Kansas. Then with Maine, New Hampshire, and Vermont. Then with Massachusetts, Connecticut, and Rhode Island. Then with Michigan, Indiana, and Ohio.

There is not much difference. Having the death penalty does not lower the murder rate. Having the death penalty does not raise it. It just does not make a difference. Therefore, it does not deter.

Your students may not all accept Sellin's study. Many of mine did not. And the ensuing discussion unwinds a whole skein of assumptions about how people behave. What we are really after is the nature of human nature and what people believe about it and whether those beliefs are based on data that can stand the light of argument.

*   *   *

A quick replay, then, of the method of setting up a lesson of inductive teaching or teaching by inquiry.

First, select your problem or the area of knowledge that you are going to teach. Try to state it as a question.

Second, collect data on that. Collect tables of statistical data, opinions, descriptions, analyses, and keep a clear record of where you got each item. Always keep a bibliography and a source reference. If you copy a table, write the reference on the same page. The reference should appear on the transparency; otherwise, they are so easily divorced.

Third, organize your data so that you can pick out one or two items as provocative starters. Look for balance, also. If there are two or three clearly stated positions, make sure that you have something from all sides. Be aware of your own bias and work hard to find arguments that you disagree with. Charles Darwin said that first. It was easy to find data in support of his own theories; he had to dig very consciously for data opposed to them.

Fourth, list on paper the skills that your class must master in order to deal with the data. Can they read tables? Understand percentages? Determine the mean, the median, and the mode? Compose a simple frequency table? Distinguish fact from opinion?

Never overestimate the ability of a class to understand simple statistics. Often, one person quickly and easily reads the table and shouts out the answers while the bulk of the class sits there relieved and grateful that no one exposed their ignorance. You must expose it, but never in a way that embarrasses. Don't assume that anyone can even do simple math or calculate percentages or do fractions. Some of them can; many cannot, and it may just be your job to teach them as the need comes up.

Remember that most readers confronted suddenly with a page of numbers just skip the whole page. Have you ever skipped? If, by wretched mischance, you are one of those frightened by figures, get a self-teaching program and learn what you have been missing. You can even do it secretly at home.

Fifth, prepare the materials so that the class can read them. Some can be duplicated or printed. Some can be typed in large letters and figures and put on a transparency. I prefer transparencies at the beginning of a lesson. That way I can make sure that we are all looking at the same thing at the same time. And in the dark, the students cannot be studying their French lesson. But transparencies are not always appropriate. They seldom are in a history class. Simple tables go well on a transparency. Long texts are better on paper.

The trick for you as a teacher to learn here is that a great many anthologies or collections of articles are like Bedau's book. They are excellent for quickly finding a whole battery of diverse viewpoints. But beware. Some such collections are loaded in one direction only. The more emotionally charged the issue, the more likely that the editor has an enormous bias. Bedau has his bias, which he clearly states.

And if you have the same bias and are unaware of it just because you are intelligent and know more than those fools who disagree with you, then you can easily drift into indoctrinating a class. Watch out. Always encourage students to seek out more data. If you use an anthology such as Bedau's, make it available.

The job is to teach students how to think, not what to think.

That is how Margaret Mead stated it in 1927. It is high time we started.

Prepared Inquiry Lessons

Much to my delight, the Population Reference Bureau once sent me a copy of *Mortality American Style*. It was written by Leon Clark (n.d.) as a teaching module about death rates and how they are influenced by life-styles.

It's a honey. The pages are full-size, ready to be copied onto transparencies. The charts are simple and easy to read. Even better, they are in order, building first a puzzle as to why one state has far higher death rates for certain diseases than does a neighboring state with similar climate, then, by adding more and more data, leading the students into an unforgettable glimpse of health, risk taking, and death. All is done by inquiry, or inductive, teaching methods. You can get it and other good materials from the Population Reference Bureau, Inc., 2213 M Street, N.W., Washington, D.C. 20037.

The interesting part of this mortality study was that its final wallop was so perfectly hidden behind simple tables of causes of death. Only when you studied them in order did you understand.

Inquiry Methods in Other Fields

Elder Network. In the spring of 1989, I joined a training group called Elder Network. We engaged in weekly training sessions for three months on counseling older people with problems. The chief requirement was that we had to be old enough to be retired as well as interested in volunteering and willing to counsel folks in trouble.

What delighted me was that the training sessions were set up largely in inquiry-oriented lessons. Our teachers, two public health nurses, Mary Doucette and Joyce Stromberg, would talk briefly about a problem and then pull a lot of examples out of the resource bank. Interestingly enough, the resource bank was the dozen elderly men and women around the table. We had lived through most of those problems or had relatives or friends who had struggled with the problems of poor diet or poverty or depression or alcohol or loneliness.

From all our combined resources, we managed to widen our understanding and to generalize about what helped and what did not. And we shared the experiences of counseling that several of our group had already done. The gist of good counseling, we learned, was that you never tell a client what to do. You manage to clarify all the options before you let the client decide. That decision requires insight into the problem plus an awareness of all possible choices.

Once again, it was the evidence-first, decision-later design.

Law. John Gowan, an attorney who lives across my street, explained the case method of teaching law. It sounded much like inquiry. The student reads a settled case with great care to discover the logic of the judge who wrote it. What were the facts? What law applied? How did it apply? If the decision was appealed and overturned, what logic did the superior judges use? The answers should all be in the decision, all written out clearly. Classes are intensely participatory.

I checked with a law student. Pat Litchy told me essentially the same: You study the case, you select which facts are crucial and which law applies and how. She thought that law school classes were far more challenging than most college classes. You could never remain passive in class.

Business and Medicine. A personal communication from Larry Daloz told me that Harvard Business School used "an elaborate form of inquiry teaching in which the 'data' are presented in a rich narrative that leads up to a climactic moment without a resolution. This becomes the take-off for class discussions in which the teacher serves as discussion leader, never becoming an 'authority.' The classic work is *Teaching and the Case Method,* by C.

Roland Christianson (1987). Related forms of 'problem-based' teaching have been developed in medical education in recent years and have caught on fast."

I crossed the street again to ask Doug McGill, a doctor at the Mayo Clinic, about medical school education. Medics have used the case method for years and years. The student gets a typical patient history and, working from that, submits a diagnosis or suggests additional testing. But Doug did suggest that there was quite a bit more to medical education than that.

Apparently, while I was puzzling around trying to learn by myself how to teach, all these bright guys could have told me. If only I had read those books earlier.

Looking Back

In organizing a lesson of inquiry, you must first begin with a problem, collect lots of relevant data, select a few provocative items, present those by transparency or on paper or orally, and let the class work over them. Data can be collected from organized anthologies, from various data banks, or from the resources of the group if they have had sufficient experience. If the data require skills in reading tables or charts, the teacher should be sure that the class knows how.

*　　　*　　　*

They have learned to criticize. They have matured by destroying some childish notions and replacing them with blueprints more securely anchored in reality. They have learned to learn on their own and to enjoy it.

What then?

The process never ends. Life is all contingent, and we must continually check our concepts against new learnings. We must grow. Only some of our mental patterns fit the new mold; hidden in the cerebral folds lurk dozens of childish fantasies waiting for us to discover and rebuild.

16

Hazards,
Reassurances,
and Joys

You pick up a book on teaching and glance through the index. Your eye catches these terms:

academic freedom	experimental program
accountability	family life education
alternative life-styles	feedback mechanism
attitude	global perspective
behavior modification	group discussion
brainstorming	growth
choosing freely	human relations
conflict	human resources
consensus	human sexuality
creative thinking	humanistic
criticism	inductive
decision making	inquiry
democracy	learning to learn
discovery	mental health

Well, that is enough to give you the idea. The above terms should alert you to the kind of book you have picked up. What kind of book is it? Do you wish to read more? Would you buy it?

That list is only part of a much longer list used by one group of school critics to detect bad books, dangerous books, books that will corrupt your children with something evil.

The National Congress for Educational Excellence, based in Dallas, once published the full list in their paper, called the *School Bell*. Their followers were urged to look through the indexes of school books and complain to the school board when they found such words. They did not have to read the book, mind you, just check the index and complain.

*   *   *

Don't get the notion that your troubles will cease when you begin to use inquiry and discovery teaching.

A few warnings:

1. My recall suffers from the universal human attitude of "old trials forgotten, happy scenes recalled." In fact, my success stories were matched by plenty of failures. The failure might come as I forgot my own rules, forgot to lead the class into doing their own thinking, forgot how scared many students can be in hazarding a guess, forgot to give a few simple lessons to build confidence, forgot to keep my approval out of the system, forgot, forgot, forgot. Lots of things can go wrong, just as they can with any system.

2. Not all teachers can handle this open-ended style of teaching. Not all can resist the impulse to approve the right answer and disapprove the wrong answer. The reason for that, of course, is that teachers are people. We follow our habits. Relearning our role takes practice and more practice, as well as the rebuilding of some strong mental patterns.

3. Not all subjects can be treated this way. To use a dictionary, you must learn the alphabet, and the simplest way is to memorize it. I was going to include the multiplication table as something best memorized, but after once seeing a Montessori teacher use cuisinaire rods to develop the concept of number, I wonder which is the better way.

Arithmetic? Algebra? Penmanship? Place geography? Many subjects might not lend themselves to this type of teaching. We need experimentation by creative teachers. Certainly, penmanship is a motor skill.

4. Don't knock memorizing. As a boy, I heard my father alone in the garden hoeing the lettuce and reciting in full the verses of "Horatius at the Bridge."

Such memorizing includes its own reward. When you see a child enjoying chess, you know that he or she has little problem learning and remembering the moves of the pieces. Later learning comes from playing, from losing, and from watching others. Many kids can rattle off thousands of facts about their sports heroes. They did not sit down to memorize; they were enthusiastic about learning.

5. A hazard lies in the vulnerability of students to a teacher who wishes to indoctrinate. This may be an entirely unconscious wish simply to help other people learn the truth as the teacher sees it. Zealots can misuse any technique.

In my own classes, I would challenge students to seek out other information, contradictory to mine. Often they would bring in very valuable stuff, sometimes irrelevant material, sometimes the original book that I was criticizing. When I tried to debunk paranormal claims, the true believers brought in magazines, tabloids, and books to prove the existence of flying saucers, ghosts, Bigfoot, extraterrestrials, and the power of apricot seeds to cure cancer.

We seem to have a whole subculture out there that has lost its original faith in science. And that's fine; science should not rest on faith. But when students substitute a faith in voodoo or astrology or palm reading or crystals, that is an opportunity for the teacher.

6. A few administrators tense up when teachers encourage students to criticize and to think for themselves and to raise bothersome questions.

One teacher in a high school English class had the students list on the board the various meanings of the word *fast* as found in the dictionary: going without food; moving quickly; taking little time, indicating time in advance of the correct time, as of a clock; allowing rapid movement, as streamlining; showing unconventional behavior; showing great energy; firmly held, as an animal in a trap; firmly tied, as a knot; closed and secured; loyal, as a fast friend; permanent, as a fast dye; deep or sound, as sleep; transmitting much light, as a fast lens; and the list went on.

Suddenly the door opened; the high school principal rushed in, saw the class studying the dictionary, bellowed approval, and told them, "Remember always that a word has one meaning and one meaning only. Never let some liar tell you that a word has two meanings. Just look it up in the dictionary and prove it."

He rushed out again, shouting over his shoulder, "Good class, good class."

Behind him, fixed fast in near shock, sat the class; the fastest to catch on lay their heads on their desks trying to hold fast to their giggles; the bulk of them stared at the teacher and at the list on the board and at the door now closed fast behind the fast-departing principal.

The teacher took a deep breath and utterly ignored the fast interruption. Later, though, he said that it was the most effective class hour he had ever taught. "Mighty fast learning. Fast meaning quick and fast meaning enduring."

7. Other hazards can come from parents who feel threatened, such as the father who taught his children to watch out for cops while he drove too fast, or from any parent whose values are questioned.

Do not undervalue some risks. Tact will get you around most of them. Strong-minded boards and superintendents and presidents can support you. Or the weak ones can let you go without support. But remember that Socrates was seventy years old when they gave him the hemlock. Just think how much good teaching you can manage before you are seventy.

8. A few teachers can utterly misuse the system by talking too much, by steering students into the "right" answers, by visible approval and disapproval that cuts out the ability of the class to grow in critical abilities, or by outright propagandizing of a pet view. The answer to that lies in the training of teachers in methods of inquiry, and that involves training in keeping your mouth shut, in smiling, and in the amiable grunt, which is also a neutral grunt.

9. Jan Streiff, a young teacher who learned this technique from me, said that she had never heard of inquiry from college

classes in educational methods. Later, she revised that. After checking her notes, she found that in one class, the professor had lectured for several minutes on the value of inquiry methods and problems versus the value of lecturing.

"You mean he *lectured* about the inquiry method?"

"Yes, all his classes were straight lectures. Never a word of discussion from us. He lectured on the value of essay questions on tests; but his tests were all objective. I guess that saved him time in correcting. But when he compared inquiry and lectures, he did say that inquiry might be much more effective. He just didn't believe what he was telling us."

If inquiry ever takes hold, such a professor must learn first. Unfortunately, he may be the last.

10. A few teachers can corrupt any discussion class into a bull session with no conclusions, no notes, no solutions. And a few of them can corrupt any class into a rehash of the last football game. One mark of a profession is the policing of its own ranks. We don't. We should.

11. The strongest opposition may come from some of the professional critics of schools who have put inductive teaching on their list of forbidden topics. Phyllis Schlafly's followers may gang up on you, through an organization called the Eagle Forum. The Texas paper called the *School Bell* may stir up some hostility. They have whole lists of thoughts that are dangerous for children and teaching methods that are to be condemned as leading to the values of humanism. A few of their dangerous terms are listed at the opening of this chapter.

We know that many students were shot in Tiananmen Square; I wonder if Deng Xiaoping was smart enough to figure out that those students were learning from teachers. What happened to them?

12. No, your days will not always be sunny and easy. You may find yourself working longer hours and reading more widely. You will learn to endure the jokes of the lecturers: "Well, did you put in another day of aimless discussion because all truth is relative?" My own private reaction was to place those critics on Perry's ladder and then smile inwardly.

Some Joys

What will happen to these students after you have taught them via inquiry/inductive/discovery methods? They will begin:

1. To develop a critical attitude.

2. To develop an attitude of reserving judgment until facts have been presented and checked.

3. To learn the process. You are not teaching the truth to be memorized; you are teaching them how to recognize truthful statements when they come across one occasionally.

4. To develop a tolerance of others and a willingness to discuss and a willingness to change their own opinion. And even to persuade you to change yours as well.

5. To develop the thinking skills needed to solve problems, to raise issues, to live in a democratic society.

6. To realize that the prime characteristic of a democratic society is that we criticize, we challenge claims, we offer alternatives. It is the most difficult form of government, the messiest form of government, and the best. Every generation must be taught the skills.

7. To develop a cooperative approach to learning rather than the rivalry of pitting student against student in endless personal competition.

8. To develop an awareness of the forces seeking to indoctrinate students with prepackaged opinions and to examine those opinions with some healthy skepticism. Here again, the student will develop the skills needed to make a democratic society work.

9. To develop an appreciation for the joy of solving a problem, detecting some humbug, recognizing propaganda.

10. To develop the skills and the methods and the habits of looking at new data and organizing them into meaningful categories in the context of group teamwork. It is those categories, those classifications that promote the retrieval of data. We can all remember things; we have trouble retrieving them, calling them up when we need them.

11. To move more completely into Piaget's fourth stage of

maturity and critical thinking by developing new patterns of thinking, new templates for processing data.

12. To move up on Perry's scheme from simple Dualism
through Relativism and into the levels of contingent Commitment.

For Parents

As a parent, you will know that your children are growing
up to be tolerant and thus more fit to live in a pluralistic and
democratic society.

As a parent, you will know that your children are developing
a healthy skepticism toward the overblown claims of advertisers and
politicians and thus more fit to live in a democratic and a competitive society.

As a parent, you will know that your children are growing
up to be intellectually ready to deal with new problems, with new
situations, without an answer in the back of the book, more ready
to live in a world that they never made.   `

As a parent, you will know that your children can cooperate
in solving problems, cooperate in gaining new knowledge, cooperate in day-to-day encounters. How we see our fellows is essential in
conflict resolution.

As a parent, you will know that your offspring will be learning the joy of learning. You can give them no better start.

For Teachers

As the teacher, you will enjoy teaching far more, and so will
your students enjoy learning. That makes it all worthwhile.

As the teacher, you will learn to encourage students to disagree with you, even when you know that you are right. You will
always have that nagging hope that this one might be the really
creative student that you can point to in later years: "I started him
off"; "I was the first to see her potential."

As the teacher, you will learn to encourage students to use
many other sources of knowledge. The library is inexhaustible. Getting them to enjoy "looking things up" in the library is one of the

best gifts you will ever give. That is best done via the tension that comes from trying to resolve the contradiction generated in a class.

As the teacher, you will learn to stifle your urge to show off that vast fund of knowledge so painstakingly acquired in years at college and years more of study. Instead, you will encourage the students to use their knowledge to curb the verbosity of the show-offs who fill the air with guff instead of knowledge.

As the teacher, you will learn to withhold instant approval and rather make the class determine the best answer. You will learn to make all sorts of noncommittal remarks. You will learn to smile, to look concerned, to keep turning to other students for confirmation and involvement. You will become the master of the amiable grunt. But you will not lose control.

As the teacher, you will have the joy of helping students move from Piaget's stage three into the maturity of stage four, capable of criticizing, of evaluating, of speculating about new hypotheses, of testing those against old data and seeking out new data. You will see students grow into the awareness that they can choose a new course of action, aware that a personal choice can affect their lives and that a national choice can affect their history.

An ancient bit of wisdom holds that the best way to learn something is to teach it. And because you are teaching tolerance and skepticism and pluralism and wide-ranging study, you may grow into that type of person yourself: tolerant, skeptical, widely read, and amiable. You may face life with reverence tinged by irony.

With the help of laryngitis, I finally learned some of these skills. How I wish that I had begun earlier.

SOME READINGS

Adler, M. *How to Read a Book*. New York: Simon & Schuster, 1972.

*Anthropology Curriculum Study Project. *Teacher Service Materials*. Washington, D.C.: American Anthropological Association, 1972.

*Bateman, W. L. *Man the Culture Builder: A Guide for Teachers, Parts I and II*. Boston: Beacon Press, 1970.

Bedau, H. A. (ed.). *The Death Penalty in America*. New York: Doubleday, 1964.

Benedict, R., and Weltfish, G. *The Races of Mankind*. Public Affairs Pamphlet #85. New York, 1943.

*Beyer, B. K. *Inquiry in the Social Studies Classroom: A Strategy for Teaching*. Westerville, Ohio, 1971.

*Bloom, B. S. (ed.). *Taxonomy of Educational Objectives: The Classification of Educational Goals. Handbook I: Cognitive Domain*. New York: McKay, 1956.

*Brookfield, S. D. *Developing Critical Thinking: Challenging Adults to Explore Alternative Ways of Thinking and Acting*. San Francisco: Jossey-Bass, 1987.

Brown, D. *Bury My Heart at Wounded Knee*. New York: Holt, Rinehart & Winston, 1970.

*Helpful books on teaching by inquiry are marked with an asterisk.

*Christianson, C. R. *Teaching and the Case Method.* Cambridge, Mass.: Harvard Business School, 1987.

*Clark, L. *Mortality American Style.* Washington, D.C.: Population Reference Bureau, n.d.

Crompton, J. *The Hunting Wasp.* Boston: Houghton Mifflin, 1955.

*Daloz, L. A. *Effective Teaching and Mentoring: Realizing the Transformational Power of Adult Learning Experiences.* San Francisco: Jossey-Bass, 1987.

Edwards, I.E.S. *The Pyramids of Egypt.* New York: Pelican, 1947.

*Fenton, E. *Studies in the Non-Western World.* New York: Holt, Rinehart & Winston, 1967.

*Fenton, E. *Teaching the New Social Studies in Secondary Schools: An Inductive Approach.* New York: Holt, Rinehart & Winston, 1967.

Gardner, H. *The Frames of Mind.* New York: Basic Books, 1983.

Gould, S. J. *The Mismeasure of Man.* New York: Norton, 1981.

Gould, S. J. *Wonderful Life.* New York: Norton, 1989.

Haley, A. *The Autobiography of Malcolm X.* New York: Grove Press, 1965.

Heiser, C. B., Jr. *From Seed to Civilization.* New York: W. H. Freeman, 1973.

*High School Geography Project and Sociological Resources for the Social Studies. *Experiences in Inquiry.* Newton, Mass.: Allyn & Bacon, 1974.

Hunter, D., and Whitten, P. *Encyclopedia of Anthropology.* New York: Harper & Row, 1976.

Johnson, E. W. *Teaching School.* New York: Walker, 1981.

Kaplan, A. *The Conduct of Inquiry.* San Francisco: Chandler, 1964.

Kroeber, T. *Ishi.* Berkeley: University of California Press, 1979.

Kuo, Z. Y. "Genesis of Cat's Responses to Rats." *Journal of Comparative Psychology,* 1930, *11* (Oct.), 1–35.

Linton, R. *The Study of Man.* East Norwalk, Conn.: Appleton-Century-Crofts, 1936.

Machiavelli, N. *The Prince.* New York: Mentor, 1952. (Originally published 1513).

*Meyers, C. *Teaching Students to Think Critically: A Guide for Faculty in All Disciplines.* San Francisco: Jossey-Bass, 1986.

*Perry, W. G., Jr. *Forms of Intellectual and Ethical Development in* *the College Years: A Scheme.* New York: Holt, Rinehart & Winston, 1970.

*Postman, N., and Weingartner, C. *Teaching as a Subversive Activity.* New York: Dell, 1969.

Richmond, P. G. *An Introduction to Piaget.* New York: Basic Books, 1971.

Ruesch, H. *Top of the World.* New York: Pocket Books, 1951.

Russell, B. *A History of Western Philosophy.* New York: Simon & Schuster, 1967.

Sharp, E. *The IQ Cult.* New York: Coward, McCann & Geoghegan, 1972.

*Spradley, J. P., and McCurdy, D. W. *The Cultural Experience: Ethnography in Complex Society.* Chicago: Science Research Associates, 1972.

Underhill, R. *Red Man's Religion.* Chicago: University of Chicago Press, 1965.

Wahlgren, E. *The Kensington Stone.* Madison: University of Wisconsin Press, 1958.

Weatherford, J. *Indian Givers: How the Indians of the Americas Transformed the World.* New York: Crown, 1988.

INDEX

ness of, 44–47; on race differences, 43–44; of readers, 55, 56; recognizing, 57; and sociology class,
48–49; of sources, 52–54; of wri-
ters, 54–55. *See also* Assump-
tions; Prejudice
Bible: and bias of reader, 55; and dis-
equilibrium, 31; and rigid beliefs,
64–67, 68–69
Bibliography slips, 190
Birds, instincts of, 86–87
Birdwatching, negative model of, 23
Black and white, and racism, 95–97
Blacks: army test scores of, 98–99;
and self-image of children, 104–
106
Blaming the victim, 101
Blood samples, insights from, 151–
152
Bloom, B. S., 118–119, 149
Boat people, impact of, 108
Boneset, 22–23
Book reports: student proofreading
of, 116; writing, 106
Bookkeeping, and inquiry method,
135
Borgia, C., 51
Bouchard, T., 93
Braidwood, R., 145, 147
Brain size, 71–72
Briggs, D., 162
Brown, D., 49, 101
Brown v. *Board of Education*, 106
Bunchberry, 21–22
Burgess shale, insights from, 162–
163
Burials, inquiries on, 15–18
Business education, inquiry method
in, 198–199
Buttoning, and norms, 155

C

Cabeza de Vaca, A. N., 149
Caesar, J., 136
Cain, T., 19–20
Calvin, J., 65
Campbell, W., 111
Carnegie Institute of Technology,

pamphlet for teaching history
from, 52
Case method, as inquiry teaching,
198–199
Catholic students, 49–50, 51, 68
Cats, and instincts, 89–90
Center for Global Education, 166
Central America, study tour in, 166–
176
Central American Parliament, 169
Central Committee for the National
Party (Honduras), 168–169
Central Intelligence Agency (CIA),
in Central America, 169, 171, 173,
175
Chambers, W., 81
Chamorro, V., 171
Cheat cards, learning from, 150
Cheating, on writing assignments,
116–117
Chicago Boy Scout Camps, nature
teaching at, 22
China, teachers and students in, 204
Chippewa Indians: and cultural
knowledge, 103–104; and fishing
rights, 107; and learning by ob-
servation, 19–20, 129
Christian Committee for Develop-
ment (Honduras), 168
Christian Socialist Party (Honduras),
169
Christian Socialist Party (Nicara-
gua), 171
Christianson, C. R., 198–199
Circle of Praxis, process of, 167
Clagett, J., 61
Clark, K., 104–105, 109
Clark, L., 197
Clark, M., 104–105, 109
Clay, H., 132
Clothing, and norms, 157–159
Cloud, R., 19–20, 103, 129
Coin, and number system, 136–137
Cole, F. C., 72
Color combinations, and norms, 156
Columbus, C., 141
Commitment stage of thinking, 38–
39, 123
Communists, hunting, 79–81